SpringerBriefs in Computer Science

Series editors

Stan Zdonik, Brown University, Providence, Rho
Shashi Shekhar, University of Minnesota, Minneapolis, Minnesota, USA
Xindong Wu, University of Vermont, Burlington, Vermont, USA
Lakhmi C. Jain, University of South Australia, Adelaide, South Australia, Australia
David Padua, University of Illinois Urbana-Champaign, Urbana, Illinois, USA
Xuemin (Sherman) Shen, University of Waterloo, Waterloo, Ontario, Canada
Borko Furht, Florida Atlantic University, Boca Raton, Florida, USA
V.S. Subrahmanian, University of Maryland, College Park, Maryland, USA
Martial Hebert, Carnegie Mellon University, Pittsburgh, Pennsylvania, USA
Katsushi Ikeuchi, University of Tokyo, Tokyo, Japan
Bruno Siciliano, Università di Napoli Federico II, Napoli, Italy
Sushil Jajodia, George Mason University, Fairfax, Virginia, USA
Newton Lee, Newton Lee Laboratories, LLC, Tujunga, California, USA

More information about this series at http://www.springer.com/series/10028

Wei-Tek Tsai · Guanqiu Qi

Combinatorial Testing in Cloud Computing

 Springer

Wei-Tek Tsai
Arizona State University
Tempe, AZ
USA

Guanqiu Qi
Arizona State University
Tempe, AZ
USA

ISSN 2191-5768   ISSN 2191-5776 (electronic)
SpringerBriefs in Computer Science
ISBN 978-981-10-4480-9   ISBN 978-981-10-4481-6 (eBook)
https://doi.org/10.1007/978-981-10-4481-6

Library of Congress Control Number: 2017955265

© The Author(s) 2017
This work is subject to copyright. All rights are reserved by the Publisher, whether the whole or part
of the material is concerned, specifically the rights of translation, reprinting, reuse of illustrations,
recitation, broadcasting, reproduction on microfilms or in any other physical way, and transmission
or information storage and retrieval, electronic adaptation, computer software, or by similar or dissimilar
methodology now known or hereafter developed.
The use of general descriptive names, registered names, trademarks, service marks, etc. in this
publication does not imply, even in the absence of a specific statement, that such names are exempt from
the relevant protective laws and regulations and therefore free for general use.
The publisher, the authors and the editors are safe to assume that the advice and information in this
book are believed to be true and accurate at the date of publication. Neither the publisher nor the
authors or the editors give a warranty, express or implied, with respect to the material contained herein or
for any errors or omissions that may have been made. The publisher remains neutral with regard to
jurisdictional claims in published maps and institutional affiliations.

Printed on acid-free paper

This Springer imprint is published by Springer Nature
The registered company is Springer Nature Singapore Pte Ltd.
The registered company address is: 152 Beach Road, #21-01/04 Gateway East, Singapore 189721, Singapore

Preface

Traditional testing faces significant complexity issues due to the increasing number of data, paths, combinations, permutations, and so on. Various testing methods have been proposed and used to improve the quality and reliability of software. As one branch of software testing, combinatorial testing (CT) is one black-box testing method to identify faults caused by the interaction of a few components. CT is considered a hard problem due to its exponential complexity: A system with 30 choice items may need to explore 2^{30} combinations and this is time- and effort-consuming.

Many approaches have been proposed in the last 40 years using various theoretical models or techniques such as Latin square, orthogonal array, covering array, machine learning. In the past 20 years, the evolutionary solutions of combinatorial testing, such as AETG, IPO, have been proposed to generate a small set of test cases that achieves 100% test coverage. However, in spite of significant progress, it is still difficult to apply CT for a system of moderate sizes such as 100 choice items. These solutions mainly focus on test coverage and not much work on fault identification.

This book proposes a computational approach to address the CT problem; instead of general purpose machine learning algorithms to learn from cases, it explores the CT structure to eliminate combinations for consideration, and the exploration can be done in a parallel manner, and the process can be done in a cloud environment where parallel processing is a standard feature. This approach allows performing CT for a system with size of 2^{40}, with $2^{2^{40}}$ combinations to consider. Thus, effectively, CT can run on a large system.

This book intends to propose a faulty location analysis solution of CT as well as review existing CT solutions. Chapter 1 reviews existing combinatorial designs and CT solutions of test case generation. Chapter 2 discusses CT practical application in cloud computing and compares existing faulty location analysis solutions in CT. Chapter 3 introduces adaptive reasoning (AR) algorithm in multi-tenancy Software-as-a-Service (SaaS) system. In the next three chapters, it describes the formal definitions of test algebra (TA), discusses the related optimizations of TA, and simulates TA in cloud environment. The last three chapters propose an integrated Testing-as-a-Service (TaaS) design with AR and TA, discuss the related testing strategies, and simulate the proposed TaaS design to solve a large-scale CT problem in cloud environment.

This book can serve as reference text for graduate students and researchers who work in combinatorial testing area. It should also be interesting to those who work in fault identification, fault location, and other related fields in testing. Practitioners may be inspired by this book in testing plan design. Due to the limitation of our knowledge, we could not provide more details in relationship between existing faults and potential faults now. But our research moves forward in fault location analysis step-by-step. You are welcome to contact us, if you have any comments and suggestions.

This work is built on many outstanding CT work in the past, and their contributions are greatly appreciated. Prof. Charles Colbourn of Arizona State University, a leading expert on CT, was a co-author of some of research papers published. Prof. Wenjun Wu of Beihang University provided the initial computing environment for us to perform computational experiments, and our great friend Tony provided 40 large servers for us to perform CT experiments on a system of 2^{50} choice items. By the way, the data generated by the 2^{50} is so large that it will take months just to transfer data.

The editors at Springer, Celine Chang and Jane Li, are always helpful. We are grateful to them for their constructive suggestions and patience. Finally, we are also indebted to our family members who suffered through the writing of this work that seems to last forever.

Beijing, China and San Jose, USA   Wei-Tek Tsai
May 2017   Guanqiu Qi

Contents

Chapter 1
Introduction

Abstract This chapter gives an introduction to software testing and cloud testing. It describes the basic concepts of combinatorial testing in detail, including Latin squares, orthogonal arrays, and covering arrays. The popular combinatorial testing algorithms, such as AETG and IPO, are discussed.

1.1 Software Testing

Software testing is an essential activity in software development to ensure the correctness of program, or software quality [52]. In general, testing is often an afterthought for a new technology, and it was not considered beforehand. Software testing uses different test cases to detect potential software bugs that cannot be identified during software development. Many testing methods have been proposed and used to increase the quality and reliability of software and systems [29, 52]. For example, black-box testing tests the functionality of an application without knowing its internal structures or workings [44] and white-box testing tests internal structures or workings of an application [49]. Conventional software testing already faces significant complexity issues as number of data, paths, combinations, and permutations that are already large (exponential).

One main challenge of software testing is to represent the variability in an expressive and practical way. Domain-specific languages, feature diagrams, and other modeling techniques are used to express variability [37].

Another challenge is to generate test cases automatically using a description of the variability to reveal faults effectively. Testing all combinations of inputs and/or configurations is infeasible in general [24, 30]. The number of defects in a software product can be large, and defects occurring infrequently are difficult to find. Testing regimes balance the needs to generate tests quickly, to employ as few tests as possible, and to represent as many of the potential faults in tests as possible.

Determining the presence of faults caused by a small number of interacting elements has been extensively studied in component-based software testing. When interactions are to be examined, testing involves a combination-based strategy [20]. *Random testing* (see [2], for example) selects each test configuration (i.e., one choice for

© The Author(s) 2017
W. Tsai and G. Qi, *Combinatorial Testing in Cloud Computing*,
SpringerBriefs in Computer Science, https://doi.org/10.1007/978-981-10-4481-6_1

each component) randomly without reference to earlier selections. *Adaptive random testing* (*ART*) algorithms use restricted random testing method to generate test suites that are as "different" as possible from one another [23]. Adaptive distance-based testing typically uses Hamming distance and uncovered combinations distance to generate combinatorial testing test suites. Parameters are ordered at random during the process of generating the next test case. Each parameter is assigned to a maximal value of the distance against the previously generated test cases [7].

1.2 Cloud Testing

Cloud computing plays an important role today. Many traditional softwares are hosted in cloud. The traditional software design has been changed, according to the new features of cloud.

- **Multi-tenancy architecture**: The software is designed to support multiple tenants to process their requirements at the same time. Each tenant shares the data, configuration, user management, and so on. Significant trade-offs exist between customization capability, security, and performance.
- **Sub-tenancy architecture**: It is another significant levels of complexity as tenant applications need to act as the SaaS infrastructure. Tenant application allows its own sub-tenant to develop applications [53]. New issues include sharing and security control, such as information flow.
- **Adaptive architecture and design**: Self-describing, self-adaptive, and tenant-aware units that can be migrated to any processors also extend the design all the way to storage and network.

Cloud also introduces new testing issues. Not only new designs of cloud software need to be tested, but also testing tenant applications need to involve SaaS infrastructure as SaaS/PaaS often provides automated provisioning, scheduling, and built-in fault-tolerant computing including migration. Test engines need to monitor all changes in tenant application, such as increased/decreased resource, process relocation, and automated recovery [33, 41]. And additional resources may be needed to perform similar relocation to ensure testing completeness. Even running the same experiments in the same infrastructure may produce different performance and behaviors.

SaaS testing is a new research topic [18, 39, 40]. It is concerned with identifying those interactions that are faulty including their numbers and locations. Furthermore, the number and location of faults may change as new components are added to the SaaS database. Using policies and metadata, test cases can be generated to test SaaS applications. Testing can be embedded in the cloud platform in which tenant applications are run [39]. Gao proposed a framework for testing cloud applications [18] and proposed a measure for testing scalability. Another scalability measure was proposed in [40].

1.3 Combinatorial Designs

The concepts of combinatorial objects are not new to testing. The use of orthogonal arrays in statistically designed experiments is discussed [22]. Then, the ideas are extended to different areas, including software testing. The combinatorial test suites are represented abstractly in mathematical and algorithmic way. A small number of test suites that cover many combinations of parameters are generated for the system under test (SUT). The following combinatorial designs are used.

1.3.1 Latin Square

A Latin square is an n*n array filled with n different symbols, each occurring exactly once in each row and exactly once in each column [46]. One classic computable formula for the number of L(n) of n*n array is $\prod_{k=1}^{n}(k!)^{\frac{n}{k}} \geq L(n) \geq \frac{(n!)^{2n}}{n^{n^2}}$ [42]. Figure 1.1 shows the 7*7 Latin square. Orthogonal Latin squares were used for testing compilers [28]. Orthogonal Latin squares were also used in the testing of network interfaces [50].

1.3.2 Orthogonal Array

An orthogonal array (OA) is an n*k matrix with run size n, factor number k, and strength t that is denoted by (n, s_i, t). Each column i has exactly s_i symbols, $1 \leq i \leq k$. In every n*k sub-array, each ordered combination of symbols from the t columns appears equally often in the rows [52]. An OA is simple if it does not contain any repeated rows [47]. An example of a 2-(4, 5, 1) orthogonal array with a strength 2 and four-level design of index 1 with 16 runs is shown in Fig. 1.2 [47]. An even distribution of all the pairwise combinations of values can be got in any two columns

Fig. 1.1 Latin square example

A	B	C	D	E	F	G
B	C	D	E	F	G	A
C	D	E	F	G	A	B
D	E	F	G	A	B	C
E	F	G	A	B	C	D
F	G	A	B	C	D	E
G	A	B	C	D	E	F

Fig. 1.2 Orthogonal array
example

1	1	1	1	1
1	2	2	2	2
1	3	3	3	3
1	4	4	4	4
2	1	4	2	3
2	2	3	1	4
2	3	2	4	1
2	4	1	3	2
3	1	2	3	4
3	2	1	4	3
3	3	4	1	2
3	4	3	2	1
4	1	3	4	2
4	2	4	3	1
4	3	1	2	4
4	4	2	1	3

in the array. Orthogonal array testing system (OATS) that contains robust testing concept uses orthogonal arrays to generate test suites for a software system [4].

1.3.3 Covering Array

A covering array (CA) is an n*k array with run size n, factor number k, and strength t denoted by (n, d_i, t) that is similar as OA. Exactly d_i symbols are in each column i, $1 \le i \le k$. Each ordered combination of symbols from the t columns appears at least once in every n*k sub-array [52]. For example, a CA with notation (9, 2^4, 3) is shown in Fig. 1.3a [1]. There are four parameters, and each one has two values that are represented in nine rows. A mixed level covering array (MCA) denoted by (n, t, k, $(v_1,\ldots, v_k)$) is also an n*k array in which the entries of the ith column arise from an alphabet of size v_i; in addition, choosing any t distinct columns $i_1,\ldots, i_t$, every t-tuple containing, for $1 \le j \le t$, one of the v_{i_j} entries of column i_j appears in columns $i_1,\ldots, i_t$, in at least one of the N rows [14]. Figure 1.3b represents a MCA with notation (12, 3, 2^3, 3^1) [1]. There are four parameters having three values and five parameters having four values to cover four-way interactions that are represented in 12 rows.

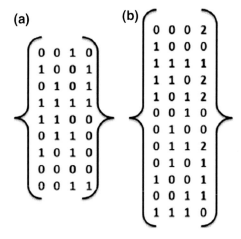

Fig. 1.3 CA and MCA examples

1.4 Combinatorial Testing

A large number of components are used in software development. Faults often arise from unexpected interactions among the components during software execution [52]. Combinatorial testing (CT) is type of software testing methods in revealing these faults. It tests all possible discrete combinations of input parameters [48]. CT can detect failures triggered by interactions of parameters with a covering array test suite generated by some sampling mechanisms. Different CT strategies are shown in Fig. 1.4. There are two main types of CT strategies. One is deterministic, and the other one is non-deterministic.

As the number of possible combinations is too large, CT needs to use a relatively small number of test suites to cover as many combinations of parameters or conditions

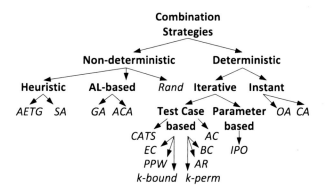

Fig. 1.4 Classification scheme for combination strategies [20]

as possible. Test coverage measures the amount of testing performed by a set of test and is used to evaluate the efficiency of testing methods.

$$test\ coverage = \frac{number\ of\ coverage\ items\ exercised}{total\ number\ of\ coverage\ items} * 100\%$$

Existing CT methods focus on test coverage and try to use the minimum test cases to reach the highest test coverage. The well-known CT algorithms are briefly discussed in the following paragraphs.

1.4.1 Covering Array for Testing

A CA of strength t is a collection of tests so that every t-way interaction is covered by at least one of the tests. CAs reveal faults that arise from improper interaction of t or fewer elements [32]. The strength of CA is important for testing. The strength t is the set of (P_i, t_i), P_i is a set of parameters, and t_i is a covering strength on P_i, for $1 \le i \le 1$ [52]. (P_i, t_i) covers all t_i-way combinations of P_i. When the strength increases, the number of test cases may increase rapidly and the testing will be more complete [52]. There are numerous computational and mathematical approaches for construction of CAs with few tests [13, 25].

If a t-way interaction causes a fault, executing a test that contains that t-way interaction must reveal the presence of at least one faulty interaction. CAs strive to certify the absence of faults and are not directed toward finding faults that are present. Executing each test of a CA, certain interactions are then known not to be faulty, while others appear only in tests that reveal faults, and hence may be faulty. At this point, a classification tree analysis builds decision trees for characterizing possible sets of faults. This classification analysis is then used either to permit a system developer to focus on a small collection of possible faults, or to design additional tests to further restrict the set of possible faults. In [51], empirical results demonstrate the effectiveness of this strategy at limiting the possible faulty interactions to a manageable number.

1.4.2 Automatic Efficient Test Generator

Combinatorial interaction testing (CIT) ensures that every interaction among t or fewer elements is tested, for a specified strength t. Among the early methods, automatic efficient test generator (AETG) [9, 11] popularized greedy one-test-at-a-time methods for constructing such test suites. In the literature, the test suite is usually called a covering array, defined as follows. Suppose that there are k configurable elements, numbered from 1 to k. Suppose that for element c, there are v_c valid options.

Table 1.1 AETG example [10]

	F1	F2	F3	F4	F5	F6	F7	F8	F9	F10	F11	F12	F13
1	1	1	1	1	1	1	1	1	1	1	1	1	1
2	1	3	3	1	3	2	2	2	3	3	1	2	1
3	3	3	1	3	2	2	2	3	3	1	2	1	1
4	3	1	3	2	2	2	3	3	1	2	1	1	3
5	1	3	2	2	2	3	3	1	2	1	1	3	3
6	3	2	2	2	3	3	1	2	1	1	3	3	1
7	2	2	2	3	3	1	2	1	1	3	3	1	3
8	2	2	3	3	1	2	1	1	3	3	1	3	2
9	2	3	3	1	2	1	1	3	3	1	3	2	2
10	3	3	1	2	1	1	3	3	1	3	2	2	2
11	3	1	2	1	1	3	3	1	3	2	2	2	3
12	1	2	1	1	3	3	1	3	2	2	2	3	3
13	2	1	1	3	3	1	3	2	2	2	3	3	1
14	1	1	3	3	1	3	2	2	2	3	3	1	2
15	3	2	2	1	2	2	1	2	2	3	3	2	2
16	2	1	2	2	3	1	2	1	3	2	3	3	2
17	2	2	2	1	3	3	3	3	1	1	1	3	1
18	2	3	3	1	2	2	3	2	1	2	2	1	3
19	1	2	3	3	2	3	3	2	1	1	1	2	2

A *t-way interaction* is a selection of t of the k configurable elements, and a valid option for each. A *test* selects a valid option for every element, and it *covers* a *t*-way interaction. When one restricts the attention to the t selected elements, each has the same option in the interaction as it does in the test.

For example, there are 13 components and each component has three options (marked as 1, 2, and 3). It would have $3^{13} = 1,594,323$ test cases. All pairwise interactions can be checked with the 19 test cases shown in Table 1.1 [10]. This is a reduction of more than 99.999% from the 1,594,323 tests required for exhaustive testing.

Another way to evaluate combination strategies is on the basis of achieved code coverage of the generated test suites [20]. Test suites generated by AETG for pairwise coverage reached over 90% block coverage [12]. AETG reached 93% block coverage with 47 test cases, compared with 85% block coverage for a restricted version of base choice (BC) using 72 test cases [8].

1.4.3 In-Parameter-Order

The in-parameter-order (IPO), as one greedy strategy of generating CAs, was proposed by Lei and Tai to extend CA in parameter order for combinatorial testing [27, 52]. The extension process starts from a pairwise test set generated for the first two parameters. It gradually extends a small CA to a large CA by adding one additional parameter each time. When an additional parameter is added, the existing pairwise test set extends in horizontal and vertical direction, respectively [27].

- *Horizontal extension*: Add a new column, when a new parameter is added.
- *Vertical extension*: Add new rows to cover those uncovered combinations by horizontal extension.

The extension process repeats until all parameters are covered.

For instance, a system has three parameters A, B, and C [26].

- Parameter A has values A1 and A2;
- Parameter B has values B1 and B2;
- Parameter C has values C1, C2, and C3.

The IPO extension process is shown in Fig. 1.5. When parameter C is added, a new column is added for the extension of parameter C. After that, two rows are added according to the extension of parameter C.

The time complexity of IPO is superior to the time complexity of AETG [20]. IPO has a time complexity of $O(v^3 N^2 \log(N))$, and AETG has a time complexity of $O(v^4 N^2 \log(N))$, where N is the number of parameters, each of which has v values [38].

1.4.4 Genetic Algorithm

A genetic algorithm (GA) is a search heuristic that mimics the process of natural selection [45]. GA is best defined as a pollution-based search algorithm based loosely on concepts from biologic evolution [34]. GA is an iterative algorithm that is used to

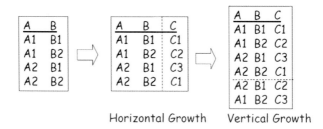

Horizontal Growth   Vertical Growth

Fig. 1.5 IPO example [26]

find CAs. In each iteration, it involves inheritance, mutation, selection, and crossover. A chromosome as a candidate solution that is distinct pairwise interaction covered by its configuration is evaluated by GA [19]. The basic AETG is extended with GA. The uncovered new t-way combinations are covered by AETG-GA. In each generation, the best chromosomes are kept and survive to the next generation [36].

1.4.5 Backtracking Algorithm

Backtracking algorithm is used to finding solutions of constraint satisfaction problems and is often implemented by a search tree. It extends a partial solution by choosing values for variables incrementally until all constraints are satisfied [52]. It abandons each partial solution as soon as it determines that the partial solution cannot possibly be completed to a valid solution [43]. Unlike brute force, backtracking checks candidate solutions, if any constraint is violated, when a variable is assigned [52].

1.4.6 Fault Detection

There are conflicting claims in the literature concerning the effectiveness of random, anti-random, and combinatorial interaction test suites at finding faults. According to [23], ART-based tests cover all t-way interactions more quickly than randomly chosen tests. At the same time, they often detect more failures earlier and with fewer test cases. According to [9, 16, 51], combinatorial interaction testing yields small test suites with high code coverage and good fault detection ability. In CIT, construction of the best test suite [21, 31] can be costly; even a solution with a small number of tests that guarantees complete coverage of t-way interactions may be difficult to produce. This has led to the frequent use of random testing [3, 17].

Schroeder et al. [35] compare the fault detection effectiveness of combinatorial interaction test suites with equally sized random test suites. Their results indicate that there is no significant difference in the fault detection effectiveness. Dalal and Mallows [15] also indicate that no matter the input size is, the numbers of interactions covered in same-sized random and combinatorial interaction test suites is similar in many cases. However, Bryce, and Colbourn [5, 6] observe that these comparisons used covering arrays that, while the best known at the time, are far from the smallest ones available. Repeating the determination of fault detection times using the smaller arrays now known changes the conclusion completely. Indeed for the situations examined in [15, 35], improving the size of the covering array used results in the random method covering a much smaller fraction of the possible faults. Moreover, covering arrays generated by a one-test-at-a-time method produced the best rate of fault detection.

1.5   Structure of This Book

With the arrival of cloud computing, the need to perform large CT to identify faulty interactions and configurations, instead of just coverage, has also arrived. At the same time, the cloud also provided significant computing resources including CPUs and storage that allow people to perform CT exercises that were not possible before. Existing CT methods mainly focus on test coverage. But high test coverage does not equal to cover more possible combinations. Actually a large number of combinations are not tested by existing CT methods. This book proposes an efficient way to explore the untested combinations in combinatorial testing.

In Chap. 2, it discusses CT in cloud computing and proposes the idea of using cloud computing resources to improve CT efficiency. The proposed solution identifies fault locations of existing test results and eliminates potential faults from testing consideration. Existing solutions of fault location analysis in combinatorial testing are discussed and compared with proposed solution.

Chapter 3 proposes an adaptive reasoning (AR) algorithm that adaptively generates test cases to identify faulty combinations in Software-as-a-Service (SaaS) system. When a new component is added to SaaS system, AR algorithm ensures any faulty combinations with new component can be identified.

Test Algebra (TA) is proposed to identify faults in combinatorial testing for SaaS applications in Chap. 4. It defines and proves the states and rules of TA. The identified faulty roots are propagated, and the potential faulty combinations are eliminated from candidate testing set.

Chapter 5 proposes a concurrent TA analysis design. The workloads are allocated into different clusters to execute TA analysis from 2-way to 6-way configurations. TA analysis algorithms and test database design are discussed.

One MapReduce design of TA concurrent execution is proposed in Chap. 6. It discusses the optimization of TA analysis. The proposed solutions are simulated using Hadoop in a cloud environment.

Chapter 7 discusses the optimization of AR algorithm. An automated test case generation method is proposed and integrated into AR algorithm to increase the efficiency of fault identification.

A Testing-as-a-Service (TaaS) design for SaaS combinatorial testing is proposed in Chap. 8. According to the workloads, the proposed design dynamically adjusts computing resources to do AR and TA analysis concurrently.

Chapter 9 proposes a large-scale TaaS system that integrates AR and TA for SaaS combinatorial testing. AR performs testing and identifies faulty interactions, TA eliminates related configurations from testing, and they can be carried out concurrently. A large size of SaaS combinations is processed by proposed system in a cloud environment.

References

1. B.S. Ahmed, K.Z. Zamli, A review of covering arrays and their application to software testing. J. Comput. Sci. **7**(9), 1375–1385 (2011)
2. A. Arcuri, L. Briand, Formal analysis of the probability of interaction fault detection using random testing. IEEE Trans. Softw. Eng. **38**(5), 1088–1099 (2012). (ISSN 0098-5589)
3. A. Arcuri, M.Z. Iqbal, L. Briand, Formal analysis of the effectiveness and predictability of random testing, in *Proceedings of the 19th International Symposium on Software Testing and Analysis, ISSTA '10* (ACM, New York, NY, USA, 2010), pp. 219–230. ISBN 978-1-60558-823-0
4. R. Brownlie, J. Prowse, M.S. Padke, Robust testing of AT&T PMX/StarMAIL using OATS. AT T Techn. J. **7**(3), 41–47 (1992)
5. R.C. Bryce, C.J. Colbourn, One-test-at-a-time heuristic search for interaction test suites, in *Genetic and Evolutionary Computation Conference (GECCO), Search-based Software Engineering track (SBSE)* (2007), pp. 1082–1089
6. R.C. Bryce, C.J. Colbourn, Expected time to detection of interaction faults. J. Comb. Math. Comb. Comput. (to appear)
7. R.C. Bryce, C.J. Colbourn, D.R. Kuhn, Finding interaction faults adaptively using distance-based strategies, in *Proceedings of the 2011 18th IEEE International Conference and Workshops on Engineering of Computer-Based Systems, ECBS '11* (IEEE Computer Society, Washington, DC, USA, 2011), pp. 4–13. ISBN 978-0-7695-4379-6
8. K. Burr, W. Young, Combinatorial test techniques: table-based automation, test generation and code coverage, in *Proceedings of the International Conference on Software Testing Analysis and Review* (West, 1998), pp. 503–513
9. D. Cohen, S.R. Dalal, M.L. Fredman, G.C. Patton, The AETG system: an approach to testing based on combinatorial design. J. IEEE Trans. Softw. Eng. **23**, 437–444 (1997)
10. D.M. Cohen, S.R. Dalal, A. Kajla, G.C. Patton, The automatic efficient test generator (AETG) system, in *Proceedings of International Conference on Testing Computer Software* (1994)
11. D.M. Cohen, S.R. Dalal, J. Parelius, G.C. Patton, The combinatorial design approach to automatic test generation. IEEE Softw. **13**(5), 83–88 (1996a)
12. D.M. Cohen, S.R. Dalal, J. Parelius, G.C. Patton, The combinatorial design approach to automatic test generation. IEEE Softw. **13**(5), 83–88 (1996b)
13. C.J. Colbourn, Covering arrays and hash families, in ed. By D. Crnkovic, V.D. Tonchev, *Information Security, Coding Theory and Related Combinatorics, volume 29 of NATO Science for Peace and Security Series–D: Information and Communication Security* (IOS Press 2011)
14. C.J. Colbourn, S.S. Martirosyan, G.L. Mullen, D. Shasha, G.B. Sherwood, J.L. Yucas. Products of mixed covering arrays of strength two. J. Comb. Des. **14**(14), 124C138 (2006)
15. S.R. Dalal, C.L. Mallows, Factor-covering designs for testing software. Technometrics **40**, 234–243 (1998)
16. S.R. Dalal, A. Jain, N. Karunanithi, J.M. Leaton, C.M. Lott, G.C. Patton, B.M. Horowitz, Model-based testing in practice, in *Proceedings of the 21st International Conference on Software Engineering, ICSE '99* (ACM, New York, NY, USA, 1999), pp. 285–294. ISBN 1-58113-074-0
17. J.W. Duran, S.C. Ntafos, An evaluation of random testing. IEEE Trans. Softw. Eng. **10**(4), 438–444 (1984). ISSN 0098-5589
18. J. Gao, X. Bai, W.-T. Tsai, SaaS performance and scalability evaluation in cloud, in *Proceedings of The 6th IEEE International Symposium on Service Oriented System Engineering, SOSE '11* (2011)
19. S. Ghazi, M. Ahmed, Pair-wise test coverage using genetic algorithms, in *Proceedings of 2003 Congress on Evolutionary Computation (CEC03)*, vol. 2 (2003), pp. 1420–1424
20. M. Grindal, J. Offutt, S.F. Andler, Combination testing strategies: a survey. Softw. Test. Verif. Reliab. **15**, 167–199 (2005a)
21. M. Grindal, J. Offutt, S.F. Andler, Combination testing strategies: a Survey. Softw. Test. Verif. Reliab. **15**(3), 167–199 (2005b)

22. A.S. Hedayat, N.J.A. Sloane, J. Stufken, *Orthogonal Arrays: Theory and Applications* (Springer, New York, 1999)
23. R. Huang, X. Xie, T.Y. Chen, Y. Lu, Adaptive random test case generation for combinatorial testing, in *COMPSAC* (IEEE Computer Society, 2012), pp. 52–61
24. C. Kaner, J. Falk, H.Q. Nguyen, *Testing Computer Software*, 2nd edn. (Wiley, New York, 1999)
25. V.V. Kuliamin, A.A. Petukhov, A survey of methods for constructing covering arrays. J. Progr. Comput. Softw. **37**(3), 121–146 (2011)
26. J. Lei, In-parameter-order: a test generation strategy for pairwise testing (2005), http://csrc. nist.gov/groups/SNS/acts/documents/ipo-nist.pdf/
27. Y. Lei, K.-C. Tai, In-parameter-order: a test generation strategy for pairwise testing, in *Proceedings of 3rd IEEE International Symposium on High-Assurance Systems Engineering, HASE '98* (1998), pp. 254–261. ISBN 0-8186-9221-9
28. R. Mandl, Orthogonal latin squares: an application of experiment design to compiler testing. Commun. ACM **28**(10), 1054–1058 (1985). ISSN 0001-0782
29. A.P. Mathur, *Foundations of Software Testing*, 2nd edn. (Pearson Education, New Jersey, 2013)
30. T. Muller, D. Friedenberg, Certified tester foundation level syllabus. J. Int. Softw. Test. Qualif. Board (2007)
31. C. Nie, H. Leung, A survey of combinatorial testing. ACM Comput. Surv. **43**(2), 11:1–11:29 (2011). ISSN 0360-0300
32. A.A. Porter, C. Yilmaz, A.M. Memon, D.C. Schmidt, B. Natarajan, Skoll: a process and infrastructure for distributed continuous quality assurance. IEEE Trans. Softw. Eng. **33**(8), 510–525 (2007)
33. G. Qi, W.-T. Tsai, W. Li, Z. Zhu, Y. Luo, A cloud-based triage log analysis and recovery framework. Simul. Model. Prac. Theory **77**, 292–316 (2017)
34. V. Rajappa, A. Birabar, S. panda, Efficient software test case generation using genetic algorithm based graph theory (2008), www.cs.uofs.edu/~bi/2008f-html/se516/peddachappali.ppt/
35. P.J. Schroeder, P. Bolaki, V. Gopu, Comparing the fault detection effectiveness of n-way and random test suites, in *Proceedings of the 2004 International Symposium on Empirical Software Engineering, ISESE '04* (IEEE Computer Society, Washington, DC, USA, 2004), pp. 49–59. ISBN 0-7695-2165-7
36. T. Shiba, T. Tsuchiya, T. Kikuno, Using artificial life techniques to generate test cases for combinatorial testing, in *Proceedings of the 28th Annual International Conference on Computer Software and Applications (COMPSAC2004)*, vol. 1 (2004), pp. 72–77
37. M. Sinnema, S. Deelstra, Classifying variability modeling techniques. Inf. Softw. Technol. **49**(7), 717–739 (2007). ISSN 0950-5849
38. K.-C. Tai, Y. Lei, A test generation strategy for pairwise testing. IEEE Trans. Softw. Eng. **28**(1), 109–111 (2002)
39. W.-T. Tsai, Q. Shao, W. Li, OIC: ontology-based intelligent customization framework for SaaS, in *Proceedings of International Conference on Service Oriented Computing and Applications(SOCA'10)* (Perth, Australia, 2010)
40. W.-T. Tsai, Y. Huang, X. Bai, J. Gao, Scalable architecture for SaaS, in *Proceedings of 15th IEEE International Symposium on Object Component Service-oriented Real-time Distributed Computing, ISORC '12* (2012)
41. W. T. Tsai, W. Li, G. Qi, Ltbd: a triage framework, in *2016 IEEE Symposium on Service-Oriented System Engineering (SOSE)* (2016), pp. 91–100
42. J.H. van Lint, R.M. Wilson, *A Course in Combinatorics* (Cambridge University Press, 1992). ISBN 978-0-521-41057-1
43. Wikipedia. Backtracking (2014a), http://en.wikipedia.org/wiki/Backtracking/
44. Wikipedia. Black-box testing (2014b), http://en.wikipedia.org/wiki/Black-box_testing/
45. Wikipedia. Genetic algorithm (2014c), http://en.wikipedia.org/wiki/Genetic_algorithm/
46. Wikipedia. Latin square (2014d), http://en.wikipedia.org/wiki/Latin_square/
47. Wikipedia. Orthogonal array (2014e), http://en.wikipedia.org/wiki/Orthogonal_array/
48. Wikipedia. All-pairs testing (2014f), http://en.wikipedia.org/wiki/All-pairs_testing/
49. Wikipedia. White-box testing (2014g), http://en.wikipedia.org/wiki/White-box_testing/

50. A. Williams, R. Probert, A practical strategy for testing pair-wise coverage of network interfaces, in *Proceedings Seventh International Symposium on Software Reliability Engineering* (1996), pp. 246–254

51. C. Yilmaz, M.B. Cohen, A. Porter, Covering arrays for efficient fault characterization in complex configuration spaces, in *Proceedings of the 2004 ACM SIGSOFT International Symposium on Software Testing and Analysis, ISSTA '04* (ACM, New York, NY, USA, 2004), pp. 45–54

52. J. Zhang, Z. Zhang, F. Ma, *Automatic Generation of Combinatorial Test Data* (Springer, New York, 2014)

53. Q. Zuo, M. Xie, G. Qi, H. Zhu, Tenant-based access control model for multi-tenancy and sub-tenancy architecture in software-as-a-service. Front. Comput. Sci. **11**(3), 465–484 (2017)

Chapter 2
Combinatorial Testing in Cloud Computing

Abstract This chapter gives an introduction to combinatorial testing. In particular, it describes the applications and challenges of combinatorial testing in cloud environment and briefly introduces solutions to address challenges. It also discusses and compares existing faulty location analysis solutions of combinatorial testing.

2.1 Combinatorial Testing in Cloud Computing

Cloud computing plays an important role today, as a new computing infrastructure to enable rapid delivery of computing resources as a utility in a dynamic, scalable, and visualized manner. Software-as-a-Service (SaaS), as a part of cloud computing among Platform-as-a-Service (PaaS) and Infrastructure-as-a-Service (IaaS), is a new software delivery model designed for Internet-based services. One single code is designed to run for different tenants. SaaS provides frequent upgrades to minimize customer disruption and enhance satisfaction. For maintenance, fixing one problem for one tenant also fixes it for all other tenants.

SaaS supports *customization*: Tenant applications are formed by composing components in the SaaS database [1, 10, 11] such as GUI, workflow, service, and data components. SaaS supports *multi-tenancy architecture (MTA)*: One code base is used to develop multiple tenant applications, so that each tenant application is a customization of the base code [9]. SaaS often also supports *scalability*, as it can supply additional computing resources when the workload is heavy.

Once tenant applications are composed, they need to be tested. However, a SaaS system can have millions of components and hundreds of thousands of tenant applications. New tenant applications are added continuously, while other tenant applications are running on the SaaS platform. New tenant applications can cause new components to be added to the SaaS system.

Combinatorial testing [3] is a popular testing technique to test a component-based application. It tests interactions among components in the configuration, assuming that each component has been tested individually. A *t-way interaction* is one that involves *t* components, and *t-way coverage* in a test suite means that every *t*-way interaction appears in at least one test configuration. Traditional combinatorial testing

© The Author(s) 2017
W. Tsai and G. Qi, *Combinatorial Testing in Cloud Computing*,
SpringerBriefs in Computer Science, https://doi.org/10.1007/978-981-10-4481-6_2

techniques focus on tests to detect the presence of faults, but fault location is an active research area. Each configuration needs to be tested, as each configuration represents a tenant application. Traditional combinatorial testing methods, such as *AETG* [4], can reveal the existence of faults by using few test cases to support t-way coverage for $t \geq 2$. But knowing the existence of a fault does not indicate which t-way interactions are faulty. When the problem size is small, an engineer can identify faults by knowing which test configurations contain a fault. However, when the problem is large, it is difficult or even impossible to identify faults if the test suite only ensures t-way coverage.

2.2   Improvements of Combinatorial Testing in Cloud Environment

The movement to Big Data and cloud computing can make hundreds of thousands of processors available. Potentially, a large number of processors with distributed databases can be used to perform large-scale combinatorial testing. Indeed, these provide significant computing power that was not available before; for example, they support concurrent and asynchronous computing mechanisms such as MapReduce, automated redundancy and recovery management, automated resource provisioning, and automated migration for scalability [8]. One simple way to perform combinatorial testing in a cloud environment is:

1. Partition the testing tasks;
2. Allocate these testing tasks to different processors in the cloud platform for test execution;
3. Collect results from the processors.

However, this is not efficient. While computing and storage resources have increased significantly, the number of combinations to be considered is still too high. Testing all of the combinations in a SaaS system with millions of components can consume all the resources of a cloud platform. Two ways to improve this approach are both based on learning from previous test results:

- Devise a mechanism to merge test results quickly, and detect any inconsistency in testing;
- Eliminate as many configurations as possible from future testing using existing testing results.

With cloud computing, test results may arrive asynchronously and autonomously. This necessitates a new testing framework. This book proposes a new algebraic system, Test Algebra (TA) [12], to facilitate concurrent combinatorial testing. The key feature of TA is that the algebraic rules follow the combinatorial structure and thus can track the test results obtained. The TA can then be used to determine whether a tenant application is faulty and which interactions need to be tested. The TA is an algebraic system in which elements and operations are formally defined. Each element represents a unique component in the SaaS system, and a set of components represents a tenant application. Assuming each component has been tested by developers, testing a tenant application is equivalent to ensuring that there is no t-way interaction faults for $t \geq 2$ among the elements in a set.

The TA uses the principle that if a t-way interaction is faulty, every $(t + 1)$-way interaction that contains the t-way interaction as a subset is necessarily faulty. The TA provides guidance for the testing process based on test results so far. Each new test result may indicate if additional tests are needed to test a specific configuration. The TA is an algebraic system, primarily intended to track the test results without knowing how these results were obtained. Specifically, it does not record the execution sequence of previously executed test cases. Because of this, it is possible to allocate different configurations to different processors for execution in parallel or in any order, and the test results are merged following the TA rules. The execution order and the merge order do not affect the merged results if the merging follows the TA operation rules.

2.3   Faulty Location Analysis in Combinatorial Testing

There are some solutions of fault location analysis in combinatorial testing. Four of them are picked for demonstration in the following paragraphs.

2.3.1   Fault Localization Based on Failure-Inducing Combinations

A spectrum-based approach to fault localization leverages the notion of an inducing combination with two novelties [6].

1. Traditional fault localization solutions only focus on the identification of inducing combinations. The proposed solution is the first effort to perform code-based fault localization based on combinatorial testing.
2. Existing spectrum-based approaches do not deal with the problem of test generation rather than assume the existence of a large number of tests that are generated randomly and/or by other methods. The proposed solution uses a systematic manner to generate a small group of tests from an inducing combination. The faults can be quickly located by analyzing the execution traces of these tests.

The idea of proposed test generation solution comes from nearest neighbor that faulty statements are likely to appear in the execution trace of a failed test but not in the execution trace of a passed test that is as similar to this failed test as possible. As the core member, one test in the group consists of the inducing combination and produces a failed test execution. As the derived member from the core member, other tests in the group execute a trace that is similar to the trace of the core member, but produce a different outcome, such as a pass execution. The spectrums of the core member and each derived member are compared to a ranking of statements in terms of their likelihood to be faulty.

There are two steps of the proposed solution.

1. *Test Generation*: It generates a group of tests. This group consists of one failed test, which is referred to as the core member, and at most t passed tests, which are referred to as the derived members. Each derived member is expected to produce a similar trace as the core member.
2. *Rank Generation*: It compares the spectrum of the core member to the spectrum of each derived member and then produces a ranking of statements in terms of their likelihood of being faulty.

The quality of top-ranked suspicious combinations affects the effectiveness of proposed solution. A suspicious combination is ranked based on the suspiciousness value of each component in the subject program. However, the top-ranked suspicious combination obtained in this way may not be a truly inducing combination.

If the generated core member does not fail, it has to pick a failed test from the initial test set as the core member. The picked failed test contains this top-ranked combination, but may not minimize the suspiciousness of its environment. This may reduce the probability for the derived members to pass.

According to the core member, the corresponding derived members are generated. The derived members pass tests that have a similar trace to the core member. If a derived member fails, it is discarded. If all the derived members fail, it has to pick a passed test from the initial test set that is similar to the core member as possible.

2.3.2   Identifying Failure-Inducing Combinations in a Combinatorial Test Set

An approach was proposed to identify failure-inducing combinations that have caused some tests to fail [5]. Given a t-way test set, it first identifies and ranks a set of suspicious combinations, which are candidates that are likely to be failure-inducing combinations. Next, it generates a set of new tests, which can be executed to refine the ranking of suspicious combinations in the next iteration. This process can be repeated until a stopping condition is satisfied.

While the proposed approach focuses on analyzing t-way combinations, it guarantees to identify inducing combinations involving no more than t parameters to be suspicious combinations. Let c be an inducing combination; it considers the following two cases.

- Case (1): c is a t-way combination. As the initial test set is a t-way test set, there is at least one test that contains c, and all test cases containing c must fail, since c is inducing. Therefore, c is identified to be a suspicious combination by the proposed approach.

- Case (2): The size of c is less than t. All t-way combinations containing c are inducing combinations and are identified to be suspicious combinations. Hence, the reduction step identifies c as a suspicious combination.

When an inducing combination involves more than t parameters, it may not appear in the initial t-way test set, and the proposed algorithm does not identify it to be a suspicious combination. The proposed approach is by nature heuristic. On the one hand, suspicious combinations that are ranked top by the proposed approach may not be truly inducing. On the other hand, truly inducing combinations may not be ranked top by the proposed approach.

The proposed approach is different from these previous techniques in that it tries to identify inducing combinations in a combinatorial test set, instead of a single failed test. On one hand, a test set contains more information than a single test. On the other hand, doing so makes it possible to identify inducing combinations that appear in different tests. Moreover, the assumption made by FIC and FIC_BS may not hold for many applications, as changing a value in a test introduces many new combinations, and assuming that all of them are non-inducing is overoptimistic.

2.3.3 Faulty Interaction Identification via Constraint Solving and Optimization

The proposed solution is an automated test result analysis technique for faulty combinatorial interactions (FCIs) based on pseudo-Boolean constraint solving and optimization techniques [14]. It uses the test results of combinatorial test suite as input and does not generate additional test cases.

The proposed approach can identify all possible solutions for the combinatorial test suite. The number of possible solutions can be used as a criterion to measure the precision of solutions. A solution is a set of suspicious FCIs. The FCI identification problem as a constraint satisfaction problem (CSP) or satisfiability (SAT) problem is formulated. It solves the formulated CSP or SAT problem to obtain corresponding FCI solutions. There are some variables in a CSP. Each of them can take values from a certain domain, and there are also some constraints. To solve a CSP, it needs to find a suitable value in the domain for each variable, such that all the constraints hold. A failing test case should match the FCI vector, and a passing test case should not match it.

This paper first assumes that there is only one failing test case in the test suite. It identifies the value combination (i.e., FCI) in this test case that can be represented by a vector like this: $< x_1, x_2, \ldots, x_k >$, where each x_i can be 0 or a value in the set D_i. When $x_j = 0$, it means that the jth attribute does not appear in the FCI. After solving the CSP, it gets the values of the variables x_i ($1 \leq i \leq k$). Then, deleting the 0s, it gets the FCI.

Since there may be many FCI solutions of the constraint satisfaction problem, it is desirable to find the optimal one according to some criterion. The minimization of FCI size is formulated as a pseudo-Boolean optimization (PBO) problem. In this case, it needs to maximize the total number of zero values of all FCIs. It follows the objective function: Minimize $\sum_i \sum_j P_{i,j,0}$ to meet passing and failing constraints.

The test suite may not be sufficient to provide enough information about the failure all the time. When the test suite is insufficient, there may be a number of possible solutions for the generated constraints. In this case, the localized FCIs may not be unique. The more possible solutions are obtained, the lower precision of each possible solution is, and the lower accuracy of FCI localization is. The proposed approach provides evidence of the trade-off between reducing the size of the test suite and enhancing its fault localization ability.

2.3.4   Characterizing Failure-Causing Parameter Interactions by Adaptive Testing

Zhang introduced a new fault characterization method called faulty interaction characterization (FIC) and its binary search alternative FIC_BS to locate one faulty interaction in a single failing test case, based on the following four assumptions [15].

- Assumption 1: The outcome of executing a test case on the software under test (SUT) is either pass or fail.
- Assumption 2: Test cases matching a faulty interaction must fail.
- Assumption 3: All parameters are independent.
- Assumption 4: All faulty interactions that appear during FIC are faulty interactions of Vs.

This paper provides a trade-off strategy of locating multiple faulty interactions in one test case. It supposes there is a set of parameters U. It uses each failing test case as a seed test case Vs. Then, it adaptively generates and executes some new test cases by modifying parameter values of Vs in U to locate the faulty interactions of the seed test case. All faulty interactions containing any parameters in U will be deactivated, and the rest faulty interactions are still active. For locating a t-way faulty interaction in the seed test case, the number of adaptive test cases is at most k (for FIC) or $t(\lceil log_2 k \rceil + 1) + 1$ (for FIC_BS), where k is the number of parameters.

Comparing to most existing methods, the proposed solution has stronger or equivalent ability of locating faulty interactions and needs smaller number of adaptive test cases for locating randomly generated faulty interactions. The proposed solution is based on the assumptions. However, those assumptions do not always hold in many practical applications. The proposed solution tries to weaken the assumptions.

- Weakening Assumption 1: In some applications, the SUT fails with multiple failure types. A solution is to use the appearance of a specific failure type instead of pass and fail.

Table 2.1 Comparisons between proposed solution and existing solutions

	Proposed AR + TA	Fault localization based on failure-inducing combinations	Identifying failure-inducing combinations in a combinatorial test set	Faulty interaction identification via constraint solving and optimization	Characterizing failure-causing parameter interactions by adaptive testing
Contribution	(1) Compare existing test results to identify the faulty roots by AR (2) Propagate the identified faulty roots to eliminate potential faults	(1) Code-based fault localization (2) Systematic manner to generate a small group of tests from an inducing combination	Identify inducing combinations in a combinatorial test set, instead of a single failed test	Identify all possible solutions for the combinatorial test suite. The number of possible solutions can be used as a criterion to measure the precision of solutions	A new fault characterization method called faulty interaction characterization (FIC) and its binary search alternative FIC_BS to locate one faulty interaction in a single failing test case
Weakness	The integrated test analysis framework depends on the existing test results. AR efficiency depends on the number of passing test results.	The quality of top-ranked suspicious combinations affects the effectiveness of proposed solution.	It is nature heuristic. On the one hand, suspicious combinations that are ranked top by the proposed approach may not be truly inducing. On the other hand, truly inducing combinations may not be ranked top by the proposed approach.	The test suite may not be sufficient to provide enough information about the failure all the time.	Based on four assumptions
Step	(1) AR analysis on existing test results (2) TA analysis	(1) Test generation (2) Rank generation	(1) Suspicious combination identification and ranking (2) Test generation	(1) Formulate FCIs as CSP or SAT problem (2) Solve the formulated CSP or SAT problem	(1) Use each faulty test case as a seed (2) Generate and execute new test cases to locate faulty interactions in seed
Feature	Asynchronous, decentralized, concurrent	Code-based, suspicious combinations' ranking	Suspicious combinations' ranking	Optimization, CSP/SAT problem solving	Binary search alternative FIC_BS

- Weakening Assumption 2: If this assumption does not hold and a test case matching one or more faulty interactions passes by coincidence, then several irrelevant
  parameters will be decided as fixed parameters of the faulty interaction under
  locating, so that FIC and FIC_BS can locate a superinteraction of the real faulty
  interaction.
- Weakening Assumption 3: Many applications have dependent parameters. A solution is to label all invalid test cases with pass. Similar to weakening Assumption 2, several irrelevant parameters will be decided as fixed parameters. So FIC
  and FIC_BS can locate a superinteraction of the real faulty interaction in this
  condition.
- Weakening Assumption 4: The concept of safe values is introduced. A safe value
  for parameter $^\wedge v_i$ is a value $s_{safe,i} \in \{1, 2, \ldots, s_i\}$ such that no-faulty interaction
  of the SUT contains the fixed parameter $^\wedge v_i$ with $v_i = s_{safe,i}$.

2.3.5 Comparisons of Existing Faulty Location Analysis Solutions

The faulty location analysis is an interesting and meaningful research topic in combinatorial testing. Existing solutions focus on different features of faults and explore
the potential faulty locations. Table 2.1 shows the comparisons between proposed
solution and existing solutions.

2.4 Related Work

Test results are used to isolate the faulty combinations that cause the software under
test to fail. Effective classification can increase efficiency [7]: The faulty combinations in scenarios where failures are not commonly observed are classified. Test
augmentation and feature selection can be used to enhance classification.

ACTS (Advanced Combinatorial Testing System), a combinatorial test generation
research tool, supports t-way combinatorial test generation with several advanced
features such as mixed-strength test generation and constraint handling [2, 13].

Most of existing CT methods use different strategies to generate test cases and
only identify faulty configurations, but do not exploit the faulty root of each configuration. Those existing solutions of faulty location analysis have different assumptions
and constraints. Our methods do not rely on whether random, anti-random, combinatorial interaction, or another type of combination-based test suite generation is
used. We focus on the task of large-scale distributed testing, analyzing, merging, and
maintaining test results in order to reduce the amount of testing needed.

References

1. X. Bai, M. Li, B. Chen, W.-T. Tsai, J. Gao, Cloud testing tools, in *Proceedings of IEEE 6th International Symposium on Service Oriented System Engineering (SOSE)* (Irvine, CA, USA, 2011), pp. 1–12

2. M. Borazjany, L. Yu, Y. Lei, R. Kacker, R. Kuhn, Combinatorial testing of acts: a case study, in *Proceedings of 2012 IEEE Fifth International Conference on Software Testing, Verification and Validation (ICST)* (2012), pp. 591–600

3. R.C. Bryce, Y. Lei, D.R. Kuhn, R. Kacker, Combinatorial testing, in *Handbook of Software Engineering Research and Productivity Technologies* (2010)

4. D. Cohen, S.R. Dalal, M.L. Fredman, G.C. Patton, The AETG system: an approach to testing based on combinatorial design. J. IEEE Trans. Softw. Eng. **23**, 437–444 (1997)

5. L.S.G. Ghandehari, Y. Lei, T. Xie, R. Kuhn, R. Kacker, Identifying failure-inducing combinations in a combinatorial test set, in *Proceedings of the 2012 IEEE Fifth International Conference on Software Testing, Verification and Validation, ICST '12* (2012), pp. 370–379

6. L.S.G. Ghandehari, Y. Lei, D.C. Kung, R. Kacker, D.R. Kuhn, Fault localization based on failure-inducing combinations, in *IEEE 24th International Symposium on Software Reliability Engineering, ISSRE 2013*, November 4–7 (Pasadena, CA, USA, 2013)

7. K. Shakya, T. Xie, N. Li, Y. Lei, R. Kacker, R. Kuhn, Isolating failure-inducing combinations in combinatorial testing using test augmentation and classification, in *Proceedings of the 2012 IEEE Fifth International Conference on Software Testing, Verification and Validation, ICST '12* (IEEE Computer Society, Washington, DC, USA, 2012), pp. 620–623. ISBN 978-0-7695-4670-4

8. W. Tsai, G. Qi, Z. Zhu, Scalable saas indexing algorithms with automated redundancy and recovery management. Int. J. Softw. Inf. **7**(1), 63–84 (2013a)

9. W.-T. Tsai, Y. Huang, Q. Shao, X. Bai, Data partitioning and redundancy management for robust multi-tenancy SaaS. Int. J. Softw. Inf. (IJSI) **4**(3), 437–471 (2010a)

10. W.-T. Tsai, Q. Shao, W. Li, OIC: ontology-based intelligent customization framework for SaaS, in *Proceedings of International Conference on Service Oriented Computing and Applications(SOCA'10)* (Perth, Australia, 2010b)

11. W.-T. Tsai, Y. Huang, Q. Shao, Testing the scalability of SaaS applications, in *Proceedings of IEEE International Conference on Service-Oriented Computing and Applications (SOCA)* (Irvine, CA, USA, 2011), pp. 1–4

12. W.-T. Tsai, C. Colbourn, J. Luo, G. Qi, Q. Li, X. Bai, Test algebra for combinatorial testing, in *Proceedings of the 2013 8th International Workshop on Automation of Software Test (AST)* (2013b), pp. 19–25

13. L. Yu, Y. Lei, R. Kacker, D. Kuhn, ACTS: a combinatorial test generation tool, in *Proceedings of 2013 IEEE Sixth International Conference on Software Testing, Verification and Validation (ICST)* (2013), pp. 370–375

14. J. Zhang, F. Ma, Z. Zhang, Faulty interaction identification via constraint solving and optimization, in *Proceedings of the 15th International Conference on Theory and Applications of Satisfiability Testing, SAT'12* (Springer, New York, 2012), pp. 186–199

15. Z. Zhang, J. Zhang, Characterizing failure-causing parameter interactions by adaptive testing, in *Proceedings of the 2011 International Symposium on Software Testing and Analysis, ISSTA '11* (ACM, New York, NY, USA, 2011), pp. 331–341

Chapter 3
Adaptive Fault Detection In Multi-tenancy Saas Systems

Abstract This chapter discusses combinatorial testing in multi-tenancy Software-as-a-Service (SaaS) system. SaaS often uses multi-tenancy architecture (MTA) where tenant developers compose their applications online using the components stored in the SaaS database. Tenant applications need to be tested, and combinatorial testing can be used. While numerous combinatorial testing techniques are available, most of them produce static sequence of test configurations and their goal is often to provide sufficient coverage such as 2-way interaction coverage. But the goal of SaaS testing is to identify those compositions that are faulty for tenant applications. In this chapter, it proposes an adaptive test configuration generation algorithm called adaptive reasoning (AR) that can rapidly identify those faulty combinations so that those faulty combinations cannot be selected by tenant developers for composition. Whenever a new component is submitted to the SaaS database, the AR algorithm can be applied so that any faulty interactions with new components can be identified to continue to support future tenant applications.

3.1 Adaptive Testing Framework

3.1.1 Learning from Earlier Test Results

The goal of testing tenant applications in the SaaS environment is to identify all the faulty configurations including any t-way interaction faults, for any $t \geq 2$, so that faulty configurations cannot be chosen by tenant developers in tenant application composition. The AR algorithm uses the earlier test results to generate new test cases to detect faults in tenant applications based on the following three principles [1, 2]:

Principle 1: When a tenant application (or configuration) fails the testing, there is at least one fault (may be more) in the tenant configuration.

Parts of this chapter is reprinted from [1, 2], with permission from IEEE.

© The Author(s) 2017
W. Tsai and G. Qi, *Combinatorial Testing in Cloud Computing*,
SpringerBriefs in Computer Science, https://doi.org/10.1007/978-981-10-4481-6_3

Principle 2: When a tenant application passes the testing, there is no-fault in the tenant configuration including all t-way interactions for any $t \geq 2$ among components in the configuration.

Principle 3: No matter what kind of k-way combination is, if it contains the faulty combinations, it must be faulty. The principle works from n-way to $(n + k)$-way $(n \geq 3)$.

The AR algorithm uses these two principles extensively:

1. If a configuration fails the testing, all of its t-way interactions will be a candidate-faulty, and thus all these t-way interactions are placed in a set of candidate-fault based on Principle 1.
2. If a configuration passes the testing, all of its t-way interactions are not faulty, and thus all of them will be placed in a set of no-fault based on Principle 2, even if some interactions have been placed in the candidate-fault set earlier.
3. If a configuration fails the testing, but after more testing, only one faulty inter-action is still left in the candidate-fault, then that interaction will be put into the final-fault set based on Principle 1. Otherwise, the configuration should not fail the testing.

Example:

Supposed that a tenant game application needs to be configured, and it has three components. They are object color, object speed, and screen color. Each component has two values as shown in Table 3.1. For each the object, color cannot be the same as the screen color otherwise players cannot identify the object position.

Suppose that the following configuration is tested: (color: blue; speed: 2; screen color: yellow). If this configuration fails the test and each component has been individually tested, one knows that at least one fault in this configuration, but the test does not which fault it is. Specifically, the following 2-way and 3-way interactions can be potential faults:

- Fault candidate 1 (2-way): (color: blue; speed: 2);
- Fault candidate 2 (2-way): (color: blue; screen color: yellow);
- Fault candidate 3 (2-way): (speed: 2; screen color: yellow);
- Fault candidate 4 (3-way): (color: blue; speed: 2; screen color: yellow).

Actual faults can be: single faults: candidates 1, 2, 3, and 4; or double faults: (1, 2), (1, 3), (1, 4), (2, 3), (2, 4), and (3, 4); or triple faults: (1, 2, 3), (1, 2, 4), (1, 3, 4), and (2, 3, 4); or even quadruple faults (1, 2, 3, 4). Any of 15 combinations can lead the configuration to fail. Thus, the system needs to consider all these 15 faulty sources.

Table 3.1 Sample of configuration

Object color	Object speed	Screen color
Blue	1	Yellow
White	2	White

Suppose another tenant configuration (color: blue; speed: 1; screen color: yellow) is tested, this time the configuration passed. Thus, according to Principle 2, all the 2-way and 3-way interactions within the configuration have no-faults. In other words, the following interactions are fault free:

2-way interactions: (color: blue; speed: 1), (color: blue; screen color: yellow), (speed: 1; screen color: yellow), and 3-way interactions: (color: blue; speed: 1; screen color: yellow).

Taking these two test results together, one can conclude that the following sources can be faulty: single faults: candidates 1, 3, 4; or double faults: (1, 3), (1, 4), (3, 4), or triple faults: (1, 3, 4), a reduction from 15 to 7 with just one additional test result. With additional testing, the actual fault source can be identified with pinpoint accuracy.

Based on the two principles, the AR algorithm will generate a test configuration without any t-way interactions in the final-fault set. It also generates candidate-faults, no-faults, and final-faults according to the observations. The algorithm is specified as follows.

A fault is a bug in the system, and a final-fault is a fault that has been detected by the AR algorithm. Thus, $|final - faultset| \leq |faultset|$. As AR executes, the number of final-faults will increase until all the faults are identified. However, the set of candidate-fault has a different behavior. As AR executes, the set of candidate-fault initially increases, and as each candidate-fault will be eliminated by further testing, the set will eventually decrease. At the end, the candidate-fault set will be empty.

Data Structures

The set of configurable components P_i and each value $P_{i,j}$ for P_i ($0 < i \leq n, 0 < j \leq P_i(\text{Max})$).

$P_i = \{P_{i,j}\}$ is set of values for component P_i ($0 < j \leq P_i(\text{Max})$).

$P_i(\text{Max})$ is the number of value in Component P_i.

$T = \{T_m\}$ is a test case that contains $\{P_{1,j}, P_{2,j}, ..., P_{n,j}\}$ ($0 < m \leq \text{TN}$), ($0 < j \leq P_i(\text{Max})$).

TN is the number of generated test cases.

The final-fault set is the list of interactions of $(P_{i,j}, P_{x,y})$ detected by AR ($0 < j \leq P_i(\text{Max}), 0 < y \leq P_x(\text{Max}), 0 < i \leq n, 0 < x \leq n, x \mathrel{!=} i$).

The candidate-fault set is the list of compositions of $(P_{i,j}, P_{x,y})$ ($0 < j \leq P_i(\text{Max}), 0 < y \leq P_x(\text{Max}), 0 < i \leq n, 0 < x \leq n, x \mathrel{!=} i$).

The no-fault is the list of compositions of $(P_{i,j}, P_{x,y})$ that will not fail the system ($0 < j \leq P_i(\text{Max}), 0 < y \leq P_x(\text{Max}), 0 < i \leq n, 0 < x \leq n, x \mathrel{!=} i$).

PM $= \{P_i\}$ is a new set of components that are added into the DB ($0 < i \leq m$).

m is the number of new components.

Pre-final-fault is the list of compositions of $(P_{i,j}, P_{x,y})$ which are generated by RA and verified by RA that they would cause the failure of system ($P_i, P_x \in P, 0 < j \leq P_i(\text{Max}), 0 < y \leq P_x(\text{Max}), 0 < i \leq n, 0 < x \leq n, x \mathrel{!=} i$).

Algorithm 1 AR Algorithm

1: **while** not all the two-way compositions are covered in test cases **do**
2:   **if** m $\geq$ TN **then**
3:     Generate the value for each $P_{i,j}$ by using AETG algorithm;
4:   **else**
5:     Generate the value randomly for each $P_{i,j}$ as an new TestCase T_m;
6:     //Update process:
7:     **if** final-fault contains the composition of $P_{i,j}$ in T_m **then**
8:       break and generate another TestCase;
9:     **end if**
10:    // To ensure that pairs of $P_{i,j}$ in final-fault would not appear in T_m;
11:    **if** T_m causes the failure in the system **then**
12:      **for** each composition of $P_{i,j}$ in T_m **do**
13:        **if** composition of $(P_{i,j}, P_{x,y})$ is not in candidate-fault and composition of $(P_{i,j}, P_{x,y})$
             is not in final-fault and composition of $(P_{i,j}, P_{x,y})$ is not in no-fault **then**
14:          Add $(P_{i,j}, P_{x,y})$ in candidate-fault;
15:        **end if**
16:      **end for**
17:    **else**
18:      **for** each composition of $P_{i,j}$ in T_m **do**
19:        **if** composition of $(P_{i,j}, P_{x,y})$ is in candidate-fault **then**
20:          Remove $(P_{i,j}, P_{x,y})$ in candidate-fault;
21:          Add $(P_{i,j}, P_{x,y})$ in no-fault;
22:        **end if**
23:      **end for**
24:    **end if**
25:    // Update the element in the final-fault list;
26:    **for** r = 0, r < m; r++ **do**
27:      **if** Tr causes the failure in the system **then**
28:        **for** each composition of $P_{i,j}$ in Tr **do**
29:          **if** there is only one $(P_{i,j}, P_{x,y})$ in candidate-fault **then**
30:            Remove $(P_{i,j}, P_{x,y})$ in candidate-fault;
31:            Add $(P_{i,j}, P_{x,y})$ in final-fault;
32:          **end if**
33:        **end for**
34:      **end if**
35:    **end for**
36:    m++
37: **end if**
38: **end while**

3.1.2   AR *Algorithm Framework*

The AR algorithm is a framework with two aspects can be customized.

Test case generation: Different algorithms can be used to generate test cases: (1) Random: random test cases except those configurations that contain final-fault interactions will be removed; (2) anti-random: instead of random, anti-random test case generation algorithm can be used where test cases that are far away from previous test cases will be selected for testing; (3) other hybrid methods such as start running AETG algorithm first to know the status of the faults, followed by random testing.

Stopping criteria: Different stopping criteria can be used to stop the execution: (1) The size of the candidate-faults sets as if the size stays zero for a large number of testing. This is a heuristic approach, as it does not guarantee correctness; (2) checking all completeness of final-fault and no-fault set, if all of the t-way interactions are either in the final-fault or no-fault set, the test is completed; (3) running AETG if the system thinks that the testing is completed and use the AETG algorithm to verify the completeness; (4) use a reasoning algorithm based on factors such as the results of previous test runs, and then followed by AETG to ensure coverage. Only the first approach is a heuristic.

AR algorithm detects 2-way interaction faults. AR algorithm that detects t-way interactions for t > 2 is omitted to save space.

3.1.3 Relationship Between Faults, Final-Faults, and Candidate-Faults

Figure 3.1 shows the relationship between faults, final-faults and candidate-faults. Region A, B, and C stand for faults, candidate-faults, and final-faults. One can see that

- Region $C = C \cap A$ (1)
- Region $B = D + E$ (2)
- Region $E = B \cap A$ (3)
- Region $D = B - E$ (4)

(1) means that all the final-faults that are output of AR algorithm are indeed faults. (2) and (3) show that a candidate-fault may not be a fault. Region D contains those candidate-faults that turn out not a fault later. Region E contains those candidate-faults that are faults after further testing. $E = B \cap A$ and $D = B - E$. Initially, both D and E are empty, and $A = C$. generation, test result evaluation, test database.

3.2 Simulation of AR Algorithm

The AR algorithm with random test case generation is simulated on a system with 10 components, and each can have 10 values or options that can be chosen by tenant developers. Thus, the total number of configurations is 10 billion, and it has 4,500 unique 2-way interactions. As the number of faults is seeded, the simulation will stop when the total number of faults is detected. This will be changed when applying the AR algorithm to test sample SaaS as in general one does not know the number of faults.

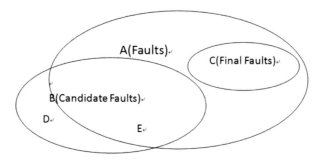

Fig. 3.1 Relationship between faults, final-faults and candidate-faults

Each simulation run uses a new random sequence of configuration compositions for evaluation. Thus, given the same simulation parameters, the results may vary slightly as a new sequence is generated for each run. However, the overall trend will be the same.

First Sample Run for Illustration

The first simulation shows the relationship between faults, candidate-faults, and final-faults using 50 2-way interaction faults, or 1.11% fault rate, and this should be considered as a high fault rate as more than 100M configurations are faulty. Table 3.2 shows the results. It showed that it takes less than 3,000 testing before all the results are obtained. Table 3.2 shows the test progression. As there are total of 10B configurations, thus only 0.00003% of configurations need to be tested before the results of all the configurations can be known.

Simulations with Different Fault Rates

We have performed further simulation with fault rates, specifically from 5, 50, 100, 200, 300 2-way interaction faults, and these represent 0.1, 1.1, 2.2, 3.3, 6.67% and of 4,500 2-way interactions, respectively. Note that about 7% fault rate should be considered as exceedingly large. As the performance of the AR algorithm will degrade when the faulty rate is high, 7% faulty rate is indeed high.

Instead of showing the progression of the AR algorithm, to reduce space, we show only the final results as shown in Fig. 3.2 where the X-axis shows the number of test cases, the Y-axis shows the final-faults/faults. With increasing test cases, more faults are identified and eventually all the faults will be identified.

If the fault rate is small, less number of test cases will be needed, but if the fault rate is high, more test cases will be needed. When there are 300 faults, about 7% of 4,500 2-way interactions, AR needs to generate 7,000 test cases to identify all the faults, about 0.00007% of 10 billion configurations.

Figure 3.3 shows that with the increasing test cases, the AR algorithm can identify more candidate-faults that turn out not real faults as all candidate faults will become either no-faults or final-faults with different fault rates. Figure 3.3 shows similar ideas but from a different perspective. Figure 3.4 shows the test configuration failure

Table 3.2 Comparison of different regions

Test cases	Candidate-faults	Final-faults	Candidate-faults But both faults	Candidate-faults + final-faults	Region C and E
10	216	0	209	216	7
20	244	0	237	244	7
30	248	0	237	248	11
50	461	0	447	461	14
100	724	0	704	724	20
150	1,036	0	1,003	1,036	33
200	1,384	0	1,339	1,384	45
250	1,270	0	1,225	1,270	45
300	1,219	0	1,171	1,219	48
350	1,108	0	1,060	1,108	48
400	995	1	946	996	50
450	960	1	912	961	50
500	799	3	753	802	50
600	659	5	614	664	50
700	394	28	372	422	50
800	178	42	170	220	50
900	74	46	70	120	50
1,000	34	48	32	82	50
2,000	0	47	0	47	50
3,000	0	50	0	50	50

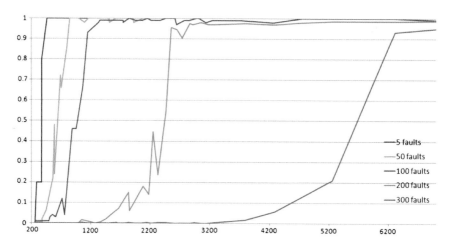

Fig. 3.2 Final-faults/faults

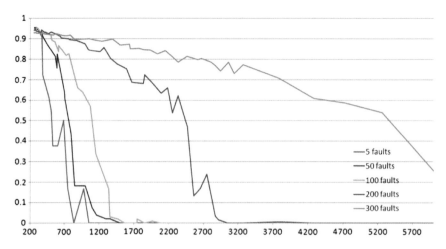

Fig. 3.3 Candidate-faults turn out not A fault/(candidate-faults + final-faults)

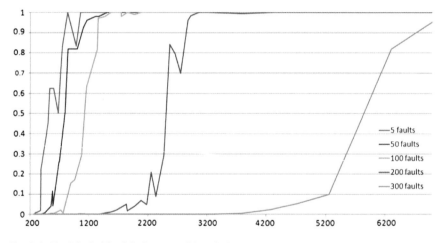

Fig. 3.4 Final-faults/(final-faults + candidate-faults)

percentage. With 300 2-way interaction faults, more than 90% of random test cases
below 6,000 failed the testing, and thus the failure rate is indeed exceedingly high.

3.3 Incremental Testing to Allow New Components

A SaaS system allows tenant developers to upload their components into the SaaS
database, and these new components can interact with the existing components causing new tenant applications to fail. The AR algorithm can be run in an incremental
manner to handle new components whenever new components are added (Fig. 3.5).

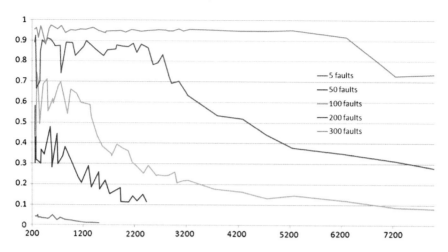

Fig. 3.5 Test configuration failure percentage

When a SaaS system starts to operate with few initial tenant components, the AR algorithm can be run and the testing results are kept in the database. When new components are added, the AR algorithm can be run, instead of starting from the scratch, using the stored test results (no-faults and final-faults) to speed up the processing. This approach is labeled as AR + PTR (previous test results).

The new test cases generation will focus on those test cases that involve new components. So, the SaaS database components will be divided into two sets, PTD (previously tested data), NTY (not test yet), and new test cases will be composed either completely from NTY or a combination of data from NTY and PTD. It is not necessary to test configuration with components from PTD, as they have been tested earlier. They can be run for regression analysis, but not for identifying new faults with new components.

Example (continued from previous section)

Suppose another two components (screen width) are added into the SaaS database, and thus there are four components. If the new configuration (color: blue; speed: 1; screen color: yellow; screen width: 500) failed in the testing, one has these 2-way, 3-way, and 4-way interactions as potential faults:

- Fault candidate 1 (2-way): (color: blue; speed: 1);
- Fault candidate 2 (2-way): (color: blue; screen color: yellow);
- Fault candidate 3 (2-way): (speed: 1; screen color: yellow);
- Fault candidate 4 (2-way): (color: blue; screen width: 500);
- Fault candidate 5 (2-way): (speed: 1; screen width: 500);
- Fault candidate 6 (2-way): (screen color: yellow; screen width: 500);
- Fault candidate 7 (3-way): (color: blue; speed: 1; screen color: yellow);
- Fault candidate 8 (3-way): (color: blue; speed: 1; screen width: 500);
- Fault candidate 9 (3-way): (color: blue; screen color: yellow; screen width: 500);

Algorithm 2 Description of AR + PTR

1: **while** not all the 2-way compositions are covered in test cases **do**
2: **if** m $\geq$ TN **then**
3:    Generate the value for each $P_{i,j}$ by using AETG algorithm;
4: **else**
5:    Generate the value randomly for each $P_{i,j}$ in component P and PM as a new TestCase T_m;
6: **end if**
7: // Update Process.
8: **if** final-fault or per-final-fault contains the composition of $P_{i,j}$ in T_m **then**
9:    Break and generate another TestCase;
10: **end if**
11: // Ensure the pairs of $P_{i,j}$ in final-fault and per-final-faults would not appear in T_m.
12: **if** T_m causes the failure in the system **then**
13:    **for** each composition of $P_{i,j}$, $P_{x,y}$ ($P_i \in (P \bigcup PM)$, $P_x \in PM$) **do**
14:      **if** composition of ($P_{i,j}$, $P_{x,y}$) is not in candidate-fault and composition of ($P_{i,j}$, $P_{x,y}$) is not in final-fault and composition of ($P_{i,j}$, $P_{x,y}$) is not in no-fault **then**
15:        Add ($P_{i,j}$, $P_{x,y}$) in candidate-fault;
16:      **end if**
17:    **end for**
18: **else**
19:    **for** each composition of $P_{i,j}$, $P_{x,y}$ ($P_i \in (P \bigcup PM)$, $P_x \in PM$) **do**
20:      **if** composition of ($P_{i,j}$, $P_{x,y}$) is in candidate-fault **then**
21:        Remove ($P_{i,j}$, $P_{x,y}$) in candidate-fault;
22:        Add ($P_{i,j}$, $P_{x,y}$) in no-fault;
23:      **end if**
24:    **end for**
25: **end if**
26: // Update the element in the final-fault list.
27: **for** r = 0, r < m; r++ **do**
28:    **if** Tr causes the failure in the system **then**
29:      **for** each composition of $P_{i,j}$, $P_{x,y}$ ($P_i \in (P \bigcup PM)$, $P_x \in PM$) in Tr **do**
30:        **if** there is only one ($P_{i,j}$, $P_{x,y}$) in candidate-fault **then**
31:          Remove ($P_{i,j}$, $P_{x,y}$) in candidate-fault;
32:          Add ($P_{i,j}$, $P_{x,y}$) in final-fault;
33:        **end if**
34:      **end for**
35:    **end if**
36: **end for**
37: m++;
38: **end while**

- Fault candidate 10 (3-way): (speed: 1; screen color: yellow; screen width: 500);
- Fault candidate 11 (4-way): (color: blue; speed: 1; screen color: yellow; screen width: 500).

If one uses the original method, one needs to verify all the 11 potential faults with new components.

However, if AR + PTR is used, according to previous test results, the configuration (color: blue; speed: 1; screen color: yellow) passes the testing, so these 2-way and 3-way interactions are not faults:

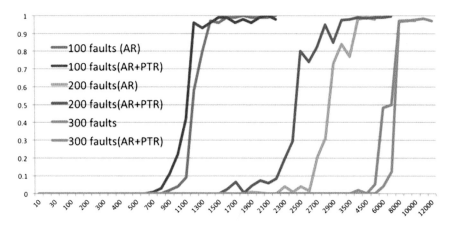

Fig. 3.6 Final-faults/faults

- Not fault 1 (2-way): (color: blue; speed: 1);
- Not fault 2 (2-way): (color: blue; screen color: yellow);
- Not fault 3 (2-way): (speed: 1; screen color: yellow);
- Not fault 4 (3-way): (color: blue; speed: 1; screen color: yellow).

Thus, one needs to verify seven interactions as four interactions are not faulty. With additional testing, the actual fault source can be identified.

Simulation Experiments of AR + PTR

Three different configurations have been simulation with $10 + 5$ components using both AR and AR + PTR. The first two cases represent those cases where relatively few components are added to an existing database, and in the last case shows that an equal amount of test cases have been added into the database. The experiments added 100, 200, and 300 faults in the $10 + 5$ components. Note that 300 faults represent a buggy situation and thus a stressed simulation.

Figure 3.6 shows that AR + PTR is more efficient than AR as AR + PTR used less test cases to cover all the faults with all the fault rates. In other words, AR + PTR takes good advantages of previously test results to identify new faults. Another interesting observation is that while $10 + 5$ has significant more components than 10 components, but it needs less test cases to obtain the results comparing the results in Sect. 4. This shows the more previously test results available, the more saving in testing effort in identifying new faults introduced.

Another practical way of reducing the testing for incremental testing is to let tenant developers to either identify those components that may be used, or exclude those components that will never be used during tenant application composition. In this way, the SaaS system will run AR + PTR with a reduced number of components to save testing effort (Figs. 3.7 and 3.8).

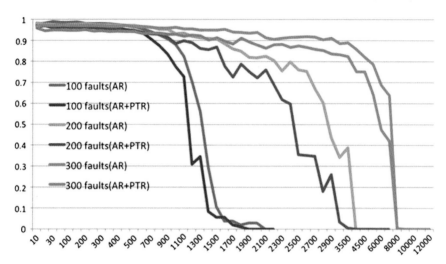

Fig. 3.7   Candidate-faults turn out not A fault/(candidate-faults + final-faults)

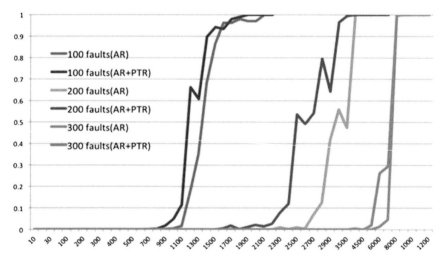

Fig. 3.8   Final-faults/(final-faults + candidate-faults)

References

1. W.-T. Tsai, G. Qi, Integrated adaptive reasoning testing framework with automated fault detection, in *Proceedings of IEEE Symposium on Service-Oriented System Engineering (SOSE2015)* (IEEE, 2015), pp. 169–178
2. W.-T. Tsai, Q. Li, C.J. Colbourn, X. Bai, Adaptive fault detection for testing tenant applications in multi-tenancy SaaS systems, in *Proceedings of IEEE International Conference on Cloud Engineering (IC2E)* (2013)

Chapter 4
Test Algebra for Concurrent Combinatorial Testing

Abstract This chapter proposes a new algebraic system, test algebra (TA) for identifying faults in combinatorial testing for Software-as-a-Service (SaaS) applications.
In the context of cloud computing, SaaS is a new software delivery model, in which
mission-critical applications are composed, deployed, and executed on cloud plat-
forms. Testing SaaS applications is challenging because new applications need to
be tested once they are composed, and prior to their deployment. A composition
of components providing services yields a configuration providing a SaaS application. While individual components in the configuration may have been thoroughly
tested, faults still arise due to interactions among the components composed, making
the configuration faulty. When there are k components, combinatorial testing algorithms can be used to identify faulty interactions for t or fewer components, for some
threshold $2 \leq t \leq k$ on the size of interactions considered. In general, these methods
do not identify specific faults, but rather indicate the presence or absence of some
fault. To identify specific faults, an adaptive testing regime repeatedly constructs and
tests configurations in order to determine, for each interaction of interest, whether
it is faulty or not. In order to perform such testing in a loosely coupled distributed
environment such as the cloud, it is imperative that testing results can be combined
from many different servers. The TA defines rules to permit results to be combined
and to identify the faulty interactions. Using the TA, configurations can be tested
concurrently on different servers and in any order. The results, using the TA, remain
the same.

4.1 Test Algebra

Let $\mathscr{C}$ be a finite[1] set of *components*. A *configuration* is a subset $\mathscr{T} \subseteq \mathscr{C}$. One is
concerned with determining the operational status of configurations. To do this, one
can execute certain tests; every *test* is a configuration, but there may be restrictions
on which configurations can be used as tests. If a certain test can be executed, its
execution results in an outcome of *passed* (*operational*) or *failed* (*faulty*).

---

[1] Parts of this chapter is reprinted from [1], with permission from IEEE.

© The Author(s) 2017
W. Tsai and G. Qi, *Combinatorial Testing in Cloud Computing*,
SpringerBriefs in Computer Science, https://doi.org/10.1007/978-981-10-4481-6_4

When a test execution yields a passing result, all configurations that are subsets of the test are operational. However, when a test execution yields a faulty result, one only knows that at least one subset causes the fault, but it is unclear which of these subsets caused the failure. Among a set of configurations that may be responsible for faults, the objective is to determine which cause faults and which do not. To do this, one must identify the set of candidates to be faulty. Because faults are expected to arise from an interaction among relatively few components, one considers t-*way* *interactions*. The t-way interactions are $\mathscr{I}_t = \{U \subseteq \mathscr{C} : |U| = t\}$. Hence, the goal is to select tests, so that from the execution results of these tests, one can ascertain the status of all t-way interactions for some fixed small value of t.

Because interactions and configurations are represented as subsets, one can use set-theoretic operations such as union, and their associated algebraic properties such as commutativity, associativity, and self-absorption. The structure of subsets and supersets also plays a key role.

To permit this classification, one can use a *valuation function* V, so that for every subset S of components, $V(S)$ indicates the current knowledge about the operational status consistent with the components in S. The focus is on determining $V(S)$ whenever S is an interaction in $\mathscr{I}_1 \cup \cdots \cup \mathscr{I}_t$. These interactions can have one of five states [1].

- **Infeasible** (X): For certain interactions, it may happen that no feasible test is permitted to contain this interaction. For example, it may be infeasible to select two GUI components in one configuration such that one says the wall is GREEN but the other says RED.
- **Faulty** (F): If the interaction has been found to be faulty.
- **Operational** (P): If an interaction has appeared in a test whose execution gave an operational result, the interaction cannot be faulty.
- **Irrelevant** (N): For some feasible interactions, it may be the case that certain interactions are not expected to arise, so while it is possible to run a test containing the interaction, there is no requirement to do so.
- **Unknown** (U): If none of these occurs, then the status of the interaction is required but not currently known.

Any given stage of testing, an interaction has one of the five possible status indicators. These five status indicators are ordered by $X \succ F \succ P \succ N \succ U$ under a relation $\succ$, and it has a natural interpretation to be explained in a moment.

4.1.1 Learning from Previous Test Results

The motivation for developing an algebra is to automate the deduction of the status of an interaction from the status of tests and other interactions, particularly in combining the status of two interactions. Specifically, one is often interested in determining $V(\mathscr{T}_1 \cup \mathscr{T}_2)$ from $V(\mathscr{T}_1)$ and $V(\mathscr{T}_2)$. To do this, a binary operation $\otimes$ on $\{X, F, P, N, U\}$ can be defined, with operation table as follows:

$$
\begin{array}{c|ccccc}
\otimes & \text{X} & \text{F} & \text{P} & \text{N} & \text{U} \\
\hline
\text{X} & \text{X} & \text{X} & \text{X} & \text{X} & \text{X} \\
\text{F} & \text{X} & \text{F} & \text{F} & \text{F} & \text{F} \\
\text{P} & \text{X} & \text{F} & \text{U} & \text{N} & \text{U} \\
\text{N} & \text{X} & \text{F} & \text{N} & \text{N} & \text{N} \\
\text{U} & \text{X} & \text{F} & \text{U} & \text{N} & \text{U} \\
\end{array}
$$

The binary operation $\otimes$ is commutative and associative (see the appendix for proofs):

$$
V(\mathcal{T}_1) \otimes V(\mathcal{T}_2) = V(\mathcal{T}_2) \otimes V(\mathcal{T}_1),
$$
$$
V(\mathcal{T}_1) \otimes (V(\mathcal{T}_2) \otimes V(\mathcal{T}_3)) = (V(\mathcal{T}_1) \otimes V(\mathcal{T}_2)) \otimes V(\mathcal{T}_3).
$$

Using the definition of $\otimes$, $V(\mathcal{T}_1 \cup \mathcal{T}_2) \succeq V(\mathcal{T}_1) \otimes V(\mathcal{T}_2)$. It follows that

1. Every superset of an infeasible interaction is infeasible.
2. Every superset of a failed interaction is failed or infeasible.
3. Every superset of an irrelevant interaction is irrelevant, failed, passed, or infeasible.

A set S is an X-*implicant* if $V(S) = $ X but whenever $S' \subset S$, $V(S') \prec$ X. The X-*implicants* provide a compact representation for all interactions that are infeasible. Indeed for any interaction $\mathcal{T}$ that contains an X-*implicant*, $V(\mathcal{T}) = $ X. Furthermore, a set S is an F-*implicant* if $V(S) = $ F but whenever $S' \subset S$, $V(S') \prec$ F. For any interaction $\mathcal{T}$ that contains an F-*implicant*, $V(\mathcal{T}) \succeq$ F. In the same way, a set S is an N-*implicant* if $V(S) = $ N but whenever $S' \subset S$, $V(S') = $ U. For any interaction $\mathcal{T}$ that contains an N-*implicant*, $V(\mathcal{T}) \succeq$ N. An analogous statement holds for passed interactions, but here the implication is for subsets. A set S is a P-*implicant* if $V(S) = $ P but whenever $S' \supset S$, $V(S') \succeq$ F. For any interaction $\mathcal{T}$ that is contained in a P-*implicant*, $V(\mathcal{T}) = $ P.

Implicants are defined with respect to the current knowledge about the status of interactions. When a t-way interaction is known to be infeasible, failed, or irrelevant, it must contain an X-, F-, or N-*implicant*. By repeatedly proceeding from t-way to $(t + 1)$-way interactions, then, one avoids the need for any tests for $(t + 1)$-way interactions that contain any infeasible, failed, or irrelevant t-way interaction. Hence, testing typically proceeds by determining the status of the 1-way interactions, then proceeding to 2-way, 3-way, and so on. The operation $\otimes$ is useful in determining the implied status of $(t + 1)$-way interactions from the computed results for t-way interactions, by examining unions of the t-way and smaller interactions and determining implications of the rule that $V(\mathcal{T}_1 \cup \mathcal{T}_2) \succeq V(\mathcal{T}_1) \otimes V(\mathcal{T}_2)$. Moreover, when adding further interactions to consider, all interactions previously tested that passed are contained in a P-*implicant*, and every $(t + 1)$ interaction contained in one of these interactions can be assigned status P.

For example, suppose that $V(a, b) = $ P and $V(a, e) = $ X. Then, $V(a, b, e) \succeq V(a, b) \otimes V(a, e) = $ X.

The valuation of the 3-way interaction (a, b, c) can often be inferred from valuations 2-way interactions (a, b), (a, c), (b, c). If any contained 2-way interaction has value F, the valuation of (a, b, c) is F, without further testing needed. But if all values of the contained 2-way interactions are P, then (a, b, c) either has valuation X or N, or it needs to be tested (its valuation is currently U).

4.1.2 Changing Test Result Status

The status of a configuration is determined by the status of all interactions that it covers.

1. If an interaction has status X (F), the configuration has status X (F).
2. If all interactions have status P, the configuration has status P.
3. If some interactions still have status U, further tests are needed.

It is important to determine when an interaction with status U can be deduced to have status F or P instead. It can never obtain status X or N once having had status U.

To change U **to** P: An interaction is assigned status P if and only if it is a subset of a test that leads to proper operation.

To change U **to** F: Consider the candidate $\mathcal{T}$, one can conclude that $V(\mathcal{T}) = F$ if there is a test containing $\mathcal{T}$ that yields a failed result, but for every other candidate interaction $\mathcal{T}'$ that appears in this test, $V(\mathcal{T}') = P$. In other words, the only possible explanation for the failure is the failure of $\mathcal{T}$.

4.1.3 Matrix Representation

Suppose that each individual component passed the testing. Then, the operation table starts from 2-way interactions, then enlarges to t-way interactions step by step. During the procedure, many test results can be deduced from the existing results following TA rules. For example, all possible configurations of (a, b, c, d, e, f) can be expressed in the form of matrix or operation table. First, we show the operation table for 2-way interactions. The entries in the operation table are symmetric, and those on the main diagonal are not necessary. So only half of the entries are shown.

As shown in Fig. 4.1, 3-way interactions can be composed by using 2-way interactions and components. Thus, following the TA implication rules, the 3-way interaction operation table is composed based on the results of 2-way combinations. Here, (a, b, c, d, e, f) has more 3-way interactions than 2-way interactions. As seen in Fig. 4.1, a 3-way interaction can be obtained through different combinations of 2-way interactions and components. For example, $\{a, b, c\} = \{a\} \cup \{b, c\} = \{b\} \cup \{a, c\} = \{c\} \cup \{a, b\} = \{a, b\} \cup \{a, c\} = \{a, b\} \cup \{b, c\} = \{a, c\} \cup \{b, c\}$. $V(a) \otimes V(b, c) = V(c) \otimes V(a, b) = V(a, b) \otimes V(b, c) = P \otimes P = U$. But $V(b) \otimes V(a, c) = V(a, b) \otimes V(a, c) = V(b, c) \otimes V(a, c) = P \otimes F = F$. As the

U	a	b	c	⋯	f	(a,b)	(a,c)	⋯	(b,c)	⋯	(e,f)
a	(a)	(a,b)	(a,c)	⋯	(a,f)	(a,b)	(a,c)	⋯	(a,b,c)	⋯	(a,e,f)
b		(b)	(b,c)	⋯	(b,f)	(a,b)	(a,b,c)	⋯	(b,c)	⋯	(b,e,f)
c			(c)	⋯	(c,f)	(a,b,c)	(a,c)	⋯	(b,c)	⋯	(c,e,f)
⋮				⋱	⋮	⋮	⋮	⋮	⋮	⋮	⋮
f					(f)	(a,b,f)	(a,c,f)	⋯	(b,c,f)	⋯	(e,f)
(a,b)						(a,b)	(a,b,c)	⋯	(a,b,c)	⋯	(a,b,e,f)
(a,c)							(a,c)	⋯	(a,b,c)	⋯	(a,c,e,f)
⋮								⋱	⋮	⋮	⋮
(b,c)									(b,c)	⋯	(b,c,e,f)
⋮										⋱	⋮
(e,f)											(e,f)

(a) Union of all Possible Interactions

⊗	a	b	c	⋯	f	(a,b)	(a,c)	⋯	(b,c)	⋯	(e,f)
a	P	F	⋯	U	U	F	⋯	U	⋯	U	
b		P	⋯	F	U	F	⋯	U	⋯	U	
c			⋯	P	U	F	⋯	U	⋯	U	
⋮			⋱	⋮	⋮	⋮	⋮	⋮	⋮	⋮	⋮
f				U	F	⋯	U	⋯	U		
(a,b)				F	⋯	U	⋯	U			
(a,c)					⋯	F	⋯	F			
⋮				⋱	⋮	⋮	⋮				
(b,c)					⋯	U					
⋮					⋱	⋮					
(e,f)											

(b) ⊗ Operation of all Possible Interactions

Fig. 4.1   3-way interaction operation table

TA defines the order of the five status indicators, the result is the highest obtained. So $V(a, b, c) = F$.

⊗	a	b	c	d	e	f
a		P	F	N	X	U
b			P	X	N	F
c				F	P	P
d					F	X
e						U
f						

4.1.4 Relationship Between Configuration and Its Interactions

One configuration contains many different interactions. The status of one configuration is composed by merging test results of all its interactions. The status of $\mathscr{T}$ can be defined as $V(\mathscr{T}) = \odot_{\mathscr{I} \subseteq \mathscr{T}} V(\mathscr{I})$, where $\mathscr{I}$ is an interaction covered by configuration $\mathscr{T}$ and $\odot$ is defined as

$\odot$	X	F	P	N	U
X	X	X	X	X	X
F	X	F	F	F	F
P	X	F	P	U	U
N	X	F	U	U	U
U	X	F	U	U	U

That is,

1. If any interaction covered by configuration $\mathscr{T}$ has a status X, then $V(\mathscr{T}) =$ X; (Otherwise, at least one interaction of configuration $\mathscr{T}$ is allowed by the specification, it cannot say that $\mathscr{T}$ is infeasible.)
2. If any interaction covered by configuration $\mathscr{T}$ has a status F and no one is infeasible, then $V(\mathscr{T}) = $ F;
3. If all interactions of configuration $\mathscr{T}$ are irrelevant or unknown, then $V(\mathscr{T}) = $ U;
4. If some interactions covered by configuration $\mathscr{T}$ have status P, the other ones have status N or U, and no one is infeasible or failed, then $V(\mathscr{T}) = $ U, so further testing is needed to determine the status of configuration $\mathscr{T}$;
5. All interactions covered by configuration $\mathscr{T}$ have status P, then $V(\mathscr{T}) = $ P.

For example, suppose that configuration $\mathscr{T}$ has three interactions $\mathscr{I}_1$, $\mathscr{I}_2$, $\mathscr{I}_3$. According to $\mathscr{T} = (\mathscr{I}_1, \mathscr{I}_2, \mathscr{I}_3)$, combinations of interaction test results can be used to determine the configuration test result. Based on the TA associative rules,

$$V(\mathscr{T}) = V(\mathscr{I}_1) \odot V(\mathscr{I}_2) \odot V(\mathscr{I}_3) \odot V(\mathscr{I}_1, \mathscr{I}_2) \odot V(\mathscr{I}_2, \mathscr{I}_3) \odot V(\mathscr{I}_1, \mathscr{I}_3) \odot V(\mathscr{I}_1, \mathscr{I}_2, \mathscr{I}_3)$$

$$= (V(\mathscr{I}_1) \odot V(\mathscr{I}_2) \odot V(\mathscr{I}_3)) \odot (V(\mathscr{I}_1, \mathscr{I}_2) \odot V(\mathscr{I}_2, \mathscr{I}_3) \odot V(\mathscr{I}_1, \mathscr{I}_3)) \odot V(\mathscr{I}_1, \mathscr{I}_2, \mathscr{I}_3)$$

$$= (V(\mathscr{I}_1) \odot V(\mathscr{I}_2) \odot V(\mathscr{I}_3)) \odot (V(\mathscr{I}_1, \mathscr{I}_2) \odot V(\mathscr{I}_2, \mathscr{I}_3)) \odot (V(\mathscr{I}_1, \mathscr{I}_3) \odot V(\mathscr{I}_1, \mathscr{I}_2, \mathscr{I}_3))$$

$$= (V(\mathscr{I}_1) \odot V(\mathscr{I}_2)) \odot (V(\mathscr{I}_3) \odot V(\mathscr{I}_1, \mathscr{I}_2)) \odot (V(\mathscr{I}_2, \mathscr{I}_3) \odot V(\mathscr{I}_1, \mathscr{I}_3)) \odot V(\mathscr{I}_1, \mathscr{I}_2, \mathscr{I}_3)$$

$$= \ldots\ldots$$

4.1.5 Merging Concurrent Testing Results

One way to achieve efficient testing is to allocate (overlapping or non-overlapping) tenant applications into different clusters; each cluster is sent to a different set of servers for execution. Once each cluster completes, test results can be merged. The testing results of a specific interaction $\mathscr{T}$ in different servers should satisfy:

- If $V(\mathscr{T}) = $ U in one cluster, then in other clusters, the same $V(\mathscr{T})$ can be either F, P, N, or U.
- If $V(\mathscr{T}) = $ N in one cluster, then in other clusters, the same $V(\mathscr{T})$ can be either F, P, N, or U.
- If $V(\mathscr{T}) = $ P in one cluster, then the same $V(\mathscr{T})$ can be either P, N, or U in all clusters;
- If $V(\mathscr{T}) = $ F in one cluster, then in other clusters, the same $V(\mathscr{T})$ can be F, N, or U.
- If $V(\mathscr{T}) = $ X in one cluster, then in other clusters, the same $V(\mathscr{T})$ can be X only.

If these constraints are satisfied, testing results can be merged. Otherwise, there must be an error in the results. To represent this situation, a new status indicator, error (E), is introduced with E $\succ$ X. We define a binary operation $\oplus$ on {E, X, F, P, N, U}, with operation table:

$\oplus$	E	X	F	P	N	U
E	E	E	E	E	E	E
X	E	X	E	E	E	E
F	E	E	F	E	F	F
P	E	E	E	P	P	P
N	E	E	F	P	N	U
U	E	E	F	P	U	U

Operation $\oplus$ is also commutative and associative; see the appendix for proofs.

Using $\oplus$, merging two testing results from two different servers can be defined as $V_{\text{merged}}(\mathscr{T}) = V_{\text{cluster1}}(\mathscr{T}) \oplus V_{\text{cluster2}}(\mathscr{T})$. The merge can be performed in any order due to the commutativity and associativity of $\oplus$. If the constraints of the merge are satisfied and $V(\mathscr{T}) = $ X, F, or P, the results can only be changed when there are errors in testing. When $V(\mathscr{T}) = $ E, the testing environment must be corrected and tests executed again after fixing the error(s) in testing. For example, when $V_{\text{cluster1}}(a, c, e) = $ X and $V_{\text{cluster2}}(a, c, e) = $ F, $V_{\text{merged}}(a, c, e) = $ X $\oplus$ F $= $ E. The error with the tests for interaction (a, c, e) must be fixed.

Using associativity of $\oplus$,

$$V_1(\mathcal{T}) \oplus V_2(\mathcal{T}) \oplus V_3(\mathcal{T})$$
$$= (V_1(\mathcal{T}) \oplus V_2(\mathcal{T})) \oplus V_3(\mathcal{T})$$
$$= V_1(\mathcal{T}) \oplus (V_2(\mathcal{T}) \oplus V_3(\mathcal{T}))$$
$$= V_1(\mathcal{T}) \oplus V_2(\mathcal{T}) \oplus V_3(\mathcal{T}) \oplus V_3(\mathcal{T})$$
$$= (V_1(\mathcal{T}) \oplus V_2(\mathcal{T})) \oplus (V_2(\mathcal{T}) \oplus V_3(\mathcal{T}))$$
$$= ((V_1(\mathcal{T}) \oplus V_2(\mathcal{T})) \oplus V_2(\mathcal{T})) \oplus V_3(\mathcal{T})$$
$$= (V_3(\mathcal{T}) \oplus V_2(\mathcal{T})) \oplus (V_3(\mathcal{T}) \oplus V_1(\mathcal{T}))$$

Thus, one can partition the configurations into overlapping sets for different servers. Conventional cloud computing operations such as MapReduce require that data should not overlap. In TA, this is not a concern.

There are six components $\mathcal{T}_1$, $\mathcal{T}_2$, $\mathcal{T}_3$, $\mathcal{T}_4$, $\mathcal{T}_5$, $\mathcal{T}_6$. They have the following relationships. $\mathcal{T}_1 = \mathcal{T}_2 \cup \mathcal{T}_3$, $\mathcal{T}_2 = \mathcal{T}_4 \cup \mathcal{T}_6$, $\mathcal{T}_3 = \mathcal{T}_4 \cup \mathcal{T}_5$.

- $V(\mathcal{T}_1) = V(\mathcal{T}_2 \cup \mathcal{T}_3) = V(\mathcal{T}_2) \otimes V(\mathcal{T}_3) = (V(\mathcal{T}_4) \otimes V(\mathcal{T}_6)) \otimes (V(\mathcal{T}_4) \otimes V(\mathcal{T}_5))$
  $= (V(\mathcal{T}_4) \otimes V(\mathcal{T}_4)) \otimes (V(\mathcal{T}_6) \otimes V(\mathcal{T}_5)) = V(\mathcal{T}_4) \otimes V(\mathcal{T}_6) \otimes V(\mathcal{T}_5)$
- $V_1(\mathcal{T}_1) \oplus V_2(\mathcal{T}_1) = V_1(\mathcal{T}_2 \cup \mathcal{T}_3) \oplus V_2(\mathcal{T}_2 \cup \mathcal{T}_3) = (V_1(\mathcal{T}_2) \otimes V_1(\mathcal{T}_3)) \oplus (V_2(\mathcal{T}_2) \otimes V_2(\mathcal{T}_3))$
- $V_x = V_1(\mathcal{T}_1) \oplus V_3(\mathcal{T}_1) = V_y = V_1(\mathcal{T}_1) \oplus V_2(\mathcal{T}_1)$

In last paragraph, it uses $\odot$ to analyze the relationship between configuration and its interactions. For example, configuration $\mathcal{T}$ has four interactions $\mathcal{I}_1$, $\mathcal{I}_2$, $\mathcal{I}_3$, $\mathcal{I}_4$. Three servers ($server_1$, $server_2$, $server_3$) are used to test these interactions. Test workloads may be assigned to different servers. The returned test results may be overlapping.

	$Server_1$	$Server_2$	$Server_3$
$\mathcal{I}_1$	assigned	assigned	
$\mathcal{I}_2$		assigned	assigned
$\mathcal{I}_3$	assigned	assigned	
$\mathcal{I}_4$	assigned	assigned	assigned

$\mathcal{I}_1$, $\mathcal{I}_2$, $\mathcal{I}_3$, and $\mathcal{I}_4$ have 2, 2, 2, and 3 test results from different servers, respectively. Total 24 possible combinations of interaction test results can be used to finalize configuration test result through dot operation defined by TA. During using $\odot$ operation, $\oplus$ can also be used to merge results from different servers. The following results can be derived according to $\oplus$ and $\odot$ rules.

$$V(\mathcal{T}) = V_{s_1}(\mathcal{I}_1) \odot V_{s_2}(\mathcal{I}_2) \odot V_{s_1}(\mathcal{I}_3) \odot V_{s_1}(\mathcal{I}_4)$$
$$= V_{s_1}(\mathcal{I}_1) \odot V_{s_3}(\mathcal{I}_2) \odot V_{s_2}(\mathcal{I}_3) \odot V_{s_1}(\mathcal{I}_4)$$
$$= V_{s_2}(\mathcal{I}_1) \odot V_{s_3}(\mathcal{I}_2) \odot V_{s_2}(\mathcal{I}_3) \odot V_{s_2}(\mathcal{I}_4)$$
$$= V_{s_2}(\mathcal{I}_1) \odot V_{s_3}(\mathcal{I}_2) \odot V_{s_1}(\mathcal{I}_3) \odot V_{s_3}(\mathcal{I}_4)$$
$$= (V_{s_1}(\mathcal{I}_1) \oplus V_{s_2}(\mathcal{I}_1)) \odot V_{s_3}(\mathcal{I}_2) \odot V_{s_2}(\mathcal{I}_3) \odot V_{s_1}(\mathcal{I}_4)$$
$$= (V_{s_1}(\mathcal{I}_1) \oplus V_{s_2}(\mathcal{I}_1)) \odot (V_{s_2}(\mathcal{I}_2) \oplus V_{s_3}(\mathcal{I}_2)) \odot V_{s_2}(\mathcal{I}_3) \odot V_{s_1}(\mathcal{I}_4) = (V_{s_1}(\mathcal{I}_1) \oplus V_{s_2}(\mathcal{I}_1)) \odot (V_{s_2}(\mathcal{I}_2) \oplus V_{s_3}(\mathcal{I}_2)) \odot (V_{s_1}(\mathcal{I}_3) \oplus V_{s_2}(\mathcal{I}_3)) \odot (V_{s_1}(\mathcal{I}_4) \oplus V_{s_2}(\mathcal{I}_4) \oplus V_{s_3}(\mathcal{I}_4))$$
$$= \ldots\ldots$$

4.1.6 Distributive Rule

To examine the distributivity of $\otimes$ over $\oplus$, the definition of $\otimes$ is extended to support E:

$\otimes$	E	X	F	P	N	U
E	E	E	E	E	E	E
X	E	X	X	X	X	X
F	E	X	F	F	F	F
P	E	X	F	U	N	U
N	E	X	F	N	N	N
U	E	X	F	U	N	U

In general, the distributivity of $\otimes$ over $\oplus$ does not hold. Instead, $V(\mathcal{T}_1) \otimes (V_1(\mathcal{T}_2) \oplus V_2(\mathcal{T}_2)) \succeq (V(\mathcal{T}_1) \otimes V_1(\mathcal{T}_2)) \oplus (V(\mathcal{T}_1) \otimes V_2(\mathcal{T}_2))$.

Equality holds when $V_1(\mathcal{T}_2) \oplus V_2(\mathcal{T}_2)$ is not E (this distributivity of $\otimes$ over $\oplus$ is proved in appendix). This can be used to further merge concurrent testing results. For example, test result of configuration (a, b, c) is infeasible that is merged by three test results from $Server_1$, $Server_2$, and $Server_3$. Similarly, configuration (b, c, d) has status P that is merged by two test results from $Server_1$ and $Server_2$. Configuration (a, b, c, d) contains configuration (a, b, c), (b, c, d), and other configurations. The test result for configuration (a, b, c, d) can be obtained by merging test results of all of these configurations. Since $V(a, b, c) = X$, no matter what status of other configuration is, configuration (a, b, c, d) always has infeasible status.

4.1.7 Incremental Development

X, F, and N interactions can be used to reduce the **TA** analysis workloads. When the number of X, F, or N interactions is large or increases, more related X, F, or N interactions will be eliminated for testing consideration.

Starting from a small SaaS, or a small subset of a SaaS, it tests the tenant applications, and develops the X, F, P, and U table gradually and incrementally.

- When a new component arrives without any association with any tenant, all interactions with any components will be marked N.
- When a new component arrives and associated with a set of tenant applications, all interactions of this component with any 2-way to 6-way interactions will be marked as U and sent to testing and **TA** analysis.
- **TA** will analyze if any of these new tenant applications need not be tested (if any of them contains any X, F, or N).
- When a tenant application is tested, all 2-way, 3-way,...., 6-way interactions with any new components will be marked P.
- If the tenant application is faulty, the faulty interaction must be identified, one possible algorithm is to use **AR** algorithm to do so.

4.2   Conclusion

This chapter proposes to address SaaS combinatorial testing using TA, which provides a foundation for concurrent combinatorial testing. The TA has two operations, and test results can have five states with a priority. By using the TA operations, many combinatorial tests can be eliminated as the TA identifies those interactions that need not be tested. Also the TA defines operation rules to merge test results done by different processors, so that combinatorial tests can be done in a concurrent manner. The TA rules ensure that either merged results are consistent or a testing error has been detected so that retest is needed. In this way, large-scale combinatorial testing can be carried out in a cloud platform with a large number of processors to perform test execution in parallel to identify faulty interactions.

Appendix

A   Commutativity of $\otimes$

The commutativity of binary operation $\otimes$.

$$V(\mathcal{T}_1) \otimes V(\mathcal{T}_2) = V(\mathcal{T}_2) \otimes V(\mathcal{T}_1).$$

Proof Since the binary operation $\otimes$ is defined as

$$
\begin{array}{c|ccccc}
\otimes & X & F & P & N & U \\
\hline
X & X & X & X & X & X \\
F & X & F & F & F & F \\
P & X & F & U & N & U \\
N & X & F & N & N & N \\
U & X & F & U & N & U \\
\end{array}
$$

Because the above matrix is symmetric on the main diagonal, the value of $V(\mathcal{T}_1) \otimes V(\mathcal{T}_2)$ is always the same as $V(\mathcal{T}_2) \otimes V(\mathcal{T}_1)$. Thus, the commutativity of $\otimes$ holds.

B Associativity of $\otimes$

The associativity of binary operation $\otimes$.

$$V(\mathcal{T}_1) \otimes (V(\mathcal{T}_2) \otimes V(\mathcal{T}_3)) = (V(\mathcal{T}_1) \otimes V(\mathcal{T}_2)) \otimes V(\mathcal{T}_3).$$

Proof We will prove this property in the following cases.

(1) At least one of $V(\mathcal{T}_1)$, $V(\mathcal{T}_2)$, and $V(\mathcal{T}_3)$ is X. Without loss of generality, suppose that $V(\mathcal{T}_1) = $ X, then according to the operation table of $\otimes$, $V(\mathcal{T}_1) \otimes (V(\mathcal{T}_2) \otimes V(\mathcal{T}_3)) = $ X $\otimes (V(\mathcal{T}_2) \otimes V(\mathcal{T}_3)) = $ X, $(V(\mathcal{T}_1) \otimes V(\mathcal{T}_2)) \otimes V(\mathcal{T}_3) = $ (X $\otimes V(\mathcal{T}_2)) \otimes V(\mathcal{T}_3) = $ X $\otimes V(\mathcal{T}_3) = $ X. Thus, in this case, $V(\mathcal{T}_1) \otimes (V(\mathcal{T}_2) \otimes V(\mathcal{T}_3)) = (V(\mathcal{T}_1) \otimes V(\mathcal{T}_2)) \otimes V(\mathcal{T}_3)$.

(2) $V(\mathcal{T}_1)$, $V(\mathcal{T}_2)$, and $V(\mathcal{T}_3)$ are not X, and at least one of $V(\mathcal{T}_1)$, $V(\mathcal{T}_2)$, and $V(\mathcal{T}_3)$ is F. Without loss of generality, suppose that $V(\mathcal{T}_1) = $ F, then according to the operation table of $\otimes$, the value of $V(\mathcal{T}_2) \otimes V(\mathcal{T}_3)$ can only be F, N, or U. So $V(\mathcal{T}_1) \otimes (V(\mathcal{T}_2) \otimes V(\mathcal{T}_3)) = $ F $\otimes (V(\mathcal{T}_2) \otimes V(\mathcal{T}_3)) = $ F, $(V(\mathcal{T}_1) \otimes V(\mathcal{T}_2)) \otimes V(\mathcal{T}_3) = $ (F $\otimes V(\mathcal{T}_2)) \otimes V(\mathcal{T}_3) = $ F $\otimes V(\mathcal{T}_3) = $ F. Thus, in this case, $V(\mathcal{T}_1) \otimes (V(\mathcal{T}_2) \otimes V(\mathcal{T}_3)) = (V(\mathcal{T}_1) \otimes V(\mathcal{T}_2)) \otimes V(\mathcal{T}_3)$.

(3) $V(\mathcal{T}_1)$, $V(\mathcal{T}_2)$, and $V(\mathcal{T}_3)$ are not X or F, and at least one of $V(\mathcal{T}_1)$, $V(\mathcal{T}_2)$, and $V(\mathcal{T}_3)$ is N. Without loss of generality, suppose that $V(\mathcal{T}_1) = $ N, then according to the operation table of $\otimes$, the value of $V(\mathcal{T}_2) \otimes V(\mathcal{T}_3)$ can only be N or U. So $V(\mathcal{T}_1) \otimes (V(\mathcal{T}_2) \otimes V(\mathcal{T}_3)) = $ N $\otimes (V(\mathcal{T}_2) \otimes V(\mathcal{T}_3)) = $ N, $(V(\mathcal{T}_1) \otimes V(\mathcal{T}_2)) \otimes V(\mathcal{T}_3) = $ (N $\otimes V(\mathcal{T}_2)) \otimes V(\mathcal{T}_3) = $ N $\otimes V(\mathcal{T}_3) = $ N. Thus, in this case, $V(\mathcal{T}_1) \otimes (V(\mathcal{T}_2) \otimes V(\mathcal{T}_3)) = (V(\mathcal{T}_1) \otimes V(\mathcal{T}_2)) \otimes V(\mathcal{T}_3)$.

(4) $V(\mathcal{T}_1)$, $V(\mathcal{T}_2)$, and $V(\mathcal{T}_3)$ are not X, F, or N. In this case, $V(\mathcal{T}_1)$, $V(\mathcal{T}_2)$, and $V(\mathcal{T}_3)$ can only be P or U. According to the operation table of $\otimes$, the values of $V(\mathcal{T}_1) \otimes V(\mathcal{T}_2)$ and $V(\mathcal{T}_2) \otimes V(\mathcal{T}_3)$ are U. So $V(\mathcal{T}_1) \otimes (V(\mathcal{T}_2) \otimes V(\mathcal{T}_3)) = V(\mathcal{T}_1) \otimes $ U $= $ U, $(V(\mathcal{T}_1) \otimes V(\mathcal{T}_2)) \otimes V(\mathcal{T}_3) = $ U $\otimes V(\mathcal{T}_3) = $ U. Thus, in this case, $V(\mathcal{T}_1) \otimes (V(\mathcal{T}_2) \otimes V(\mathcal{T}_3)) = (V(\mathcal{T}_1) \otimes V(\mathcal{T}_2)) \otimes V(\mathcal{T}_3)$.

Quisque ullamcorper placerat ipsum. Cras nibh. Morbi vel justo vitae lacus tincidunt ultrices. Lorem ipsum dolor sit amet, consectetuer adipiscing elit. In hac habitasse platea dictumst. Integer tempus convallis augue. Etiam facilisis. Nunc elementum fermentum wisi. Aenean placerat. Ut imperdiet, enim sed gravida sollicitudin, felis odio placerat quam, ac pulvinar elit purus eget enim. Nunc vitae tortor. Proin tempus nibh sit amet nisl. Vivamus quis tortor vitae risus porta vehicula.

C Commutativity of $\oplus$

The commutativity of binary operation $\oplus$.

$$V_1(\mathcal{T}) \oplus V_2(\mathcal{T}) = V_2(\mathcal{T}) \oplus V_1(\mathcal{T}).$$

Proof Since the binary operation $\oplus$ is defined as

$\oplus$	E	X	F	P	N	U
E	E	E	E	E	E	E
X	E	X	E	E	E	E
F	E	E	F	E	F	F
P	E	E	E	P	P	P
N	E	E	F	P	N	U
U	E	E	F	P	U	U

Because the above matrix is symmetric on the main diagonal, the value of $V_1(\mathcal{T}) \oplus V_2(\mathcal{T})$ is always the same as $V_2(\mathcal{T}) \oplus V_1(\mathcal{T})$. Thus, the commutativity of $\otimes$ holds.

Quisque ullamcorper placerat ipsum. Cras nibh. Morbi vel justo vitae lacus tincidunt ultrices. Lorem ipsum dolor sit amet, consectetuer adipiscing elit. In hac habitasse platea dictumst. Integer tempus convallis augue. Etiam facilisis. Nunc elementum fermentum wisi. Aenean placerat. Ut imperdiet, enim sed gravida sollicitudin, felis odio placerat quam, ac pulvinar elit purus eget enim. Nunc vitae tortor. Proin tempus nibh sit amet nisl. Vivamus quis tortor vitae risus porta vehicula.

D   Associativity of $\oplus$

The associativity of binary operation $\oplus$.

$$V_1(\mathcal{T}) \oplus (V_2(\mathcal{T}) \oplus V_3(\mathcal{T})) = (V_1(\mathcal{T}) \oplus V_2(\mathcal{T})) \oplus V_3(\mathcal{T}).$$

Proof We will prove this property in the following cases.

(1) One of $V_1(\mathcal{T})$, $V_2(\mathcal{T})$, and $V_3(\mathcal{T})$ is E. Without loss of generality, suppose that $V_1(\mathcal{T}) = $ E, then according to the operation table of $\oplus$, $V_1(\mathcal{T}) \oplus (V_2(\mathcal{T}) \oplus V_3(\mathcal{T})) = E \otimes (V_2(\mathcal{T}) \oplus V_3(\mathcal{T})) = E$, $(V_1(\mathcal{T}) \oplus V_2(\mathcal{T})) \oplus V_3(\mathcal{T}) = (E \oplus V_2(\mathcal{T})) \oplus V_3(\mathcal{T}) = E \oplus V_3(\mathcal{T}) = E$. Thus, in this case, $V_1(\mathcal{T}) \oplus (V_2(\mathcal{T}) \oplus V_3(\mathcal{T})) = (V_1(\mathcal{T}) \oplus V_2(\mathcal{T})) \oplus V_3(\mathcal{T})$.

(2) $V_1(\mathcal{T})$, $V_2(\mathcal{T})$, and $V_3(\mathcal{T})$ are not E, and there is a pair of $V_1(\mathcal{T})$, $V_2(\mathcal{T})$, and $V_3(\mathcal{T})$ does not satisfy the constrains. Without loss of generality, suppose that $V_1(\mathcal{T})$ and $V_2(\mathcal{T})$ does not satisfy the constrains, then according to the operation table of $\oplus$, $V_1(\mathcal{T}) \oplus V_2(\mathcal{T}) = E$. So $(V_1(\mathcal{T}) \oplus V_2(\mathcal{T})) \oplus V_3(\mathcal{T}) = E \oplus V_3(\mathcal{T}) = E$. Since $V_1(\mathcal{T})$ and $V_2(\mathcal{T})$ do not satisfy the constrains, there can be two cases: (a) one of them is X and the other is not, or (b) one of them is P and the other is F.

(a) If $V_1(\mathscr{T}) = $ X, then $V_2(\mathscr{T}) \oplus V_3(\mathscr{T})$ cannot be X because $V_2(\mathscr{T})$ cannot be X. Thus, $V_1(\mathscr{T}) \oplus (V_2(\mathscr{T}) \oplus V_3(\mathscr{T})) = $ E. If $V_2(\mathscr{T}) = $ X, then $V_2(\mathscr{T}) \oplus V_3(\mathscr{T}) \neq $ X can only be E or X. Since $V_1(\mathscr{T})$ cannot be X, $V_1(\mathscr{T}) \oplus (V_2(\mathscr{T}) \oplus V_3(\mathscr{T})) = $ E.

(b) If $V_1(\mathscr{T}) = $ P and $V_2(\mathscr{T}) = $ F, then $V_2(\mathscr{T}) \oplus V_3(\mathscr{T})$ can only be E or F. Thus, $V_1(\mathscr{T}) \oplus (V_2(\mathscr{T}) \oplus V_3(\mathscr{T})) = $ E. If $V_1(\mathscr{T}) = $ F and $V_2(\mathscr{T}) = $ P, then $V_2(\mathscr{T}) \oplus V_3(\mathscr{T})$ can only be E or P. Thus, $V_1(\mathscr{T}) \oplus (V_2(\mathscr{T}) \oplus V_3(\mathscr{T})) = $ E.

Thus, in this case, $V_1(\mathscr{T}) \oplus (V_2(\mathscr{T}) \oplus V_3(\mathscr{T})) = (V_1(\mathscr{T}) \oplus V_2(\mathscr{T})) \oplus V_3(\mathscr{T})$.

(3) $V_1(\mathscr{T})$, $V_2(\mathscr{T})$, and $V_3(\mathscr{T})$ are not E, and $V_1(\mathscr{T})$, $V_2(\mathscr{T})$, and $V_3(\mathscr{T})$ satisfy the constrains.

(a) One of $V_1(\mathscr{T})$, $V_2(\mathscr{T})$, and $V_3(\mathscr{T})$ is X. Without loss of generality, suppose that $V_1(\mathscr{T}) = $ X, then $V_2(\mathscr{T}) = V_3(\mathscr{T}) = $ X. So $V_1(\mathscr{T}) \oplus (V_2(\mathscr{T}) \oplus V_3(\mathscr{T})) = $ X$\oplus$(X$\oplus$X) $= $ X$\oplus$X $= $ X and $(V_1(\mathscr{T})\oplus V_2(\mathscr{T}))\oplus V_3(\mathscr{T}) = $ (X$\oplus$X)$\oplus$X $= $ X$\oplus$X $= $ X.

(b) $V_1(\mathscr{T})$, $V_2(\mathscr{T})$, and $V_3(\mathscr{T})$ are not X, and one of $V_1(\mathscr{T})$, $V_2(\mathscr{T})$, and $V_3(\mathscr{T})$ is F. Without loss of generality, suppose that $V_1(\mathscr{T}) = $ F, then $V_2(\mathscr{T})$ and $V_3(\mathscr{T})$ can only be F, N, or U. According to operation table of $\oplus$, $V_2(\mathscr{T}) \oplus V_3(\mathscr{T})$ can only be F, N, or U, and $V_1(\mathscr{T}) \oplus V_2(\mathscr{T})$ can only be F. So $V_1(\mathscr{T}) \oplus (V_2(\mathscr{T}) \oplus V_3(\mathscr{T})) = $ F $\oplus (V_2(\mathscr{T}) \oplus V_3(\mathscr{T})) = $ F and $(V_1(\mathscr{T}) \oplus V_2(\mathscr{T})) \oplus V_3(\mathscr{T}) = $ F $\oplus V_3(\mathscr{T}) = $ F.

(c) $V_1(\mathscr{T})$, $V_2(\mathscr{T})$, and $V_3(\mathscr{T})$ are not X or F, and one of $V_1(\mathscr{T})$, $V_2(\mathscr{T})$, and $V_3(\mathscr{T})$ is P. Without loss of generality, suppose that $V_1(\mathscr{T}) = $ P, then $V_2(\mathscr{T})$ and $V_3(\mathscr{T})$ can only be P, N, or U. According to operation table of $\oplus$, $V_2(\mathscr{T}) \oplus V_3(\mathscr{T})$ can only be P, N, or U, and $V_1(\mathscr{T}) \oplus V_2(\mathscr{T})$ can only be F. So $V_1(\mathscr{T}) \oplus (V_2(\mathscr{T}) \oplus V_3(\mathscr{T})) = $ P $\oplus (V_2(\mathscr{T}) \oplus V_3(\mathscr{T})) = $ P and $(V_1(\mathscr{T}) \oplus V_2(\mathscr{T})) \oplus V_3(\mathscr{T}) = $ P $\oplus V_3(\mathscr{T}) = $ P.

(d) $V_1(\mathscr{T})$, $V_2(\mathscr{T})$, and $V_3(\mathscr{T})$ are not X, F, or P, and one of $V_1(\mathscr{T})$, $V_2(\mathscr{T})$, and $V_3(\mathscr{T})$ is U. Without loss of generality, suppose that $V_1(\mathscr{T}) = $ U, then $V_2(\mathscr{T})$ and $V_3(\mathscr{T})$ can only be N or U. According to operation table of $\oplus$, $V_2(\mathscr{T}) \oplus V_3(\mathscr{T})$ can only be N or U, and $V_1(\mathscr{T})\oplus V_2(\mathscr{T})$ can only be U. So $V_1(\mathscr{T})\oplus(V_2(\mathscr{T})\oplus V_3(\mathscr{T})) = $ U $\oplus (V_2(\mathscr{T}) \oplus V_3(\mathscr{T})) = $ U and $(V_1(\mathscr{T}) \oplus V_2(\mathscr{T})) \oplus V_3(\mathscr{T}) = $ U $\oplus V_3(\mathscr{T}) = $ U.

(e) $V_1(\mathscr{T})$, $V_2(\mathscr{T})$, and $V_3(\mathscr{T})$ are N. $V_1(\mathscr{T})\oplus(V_2(\mathscr{T})\oplus V_3(\mathscr{T})) = $ N$\oplus$(N$\oplus$N) $= $ N $\oplus$ N $= $ N and $(V_1(\mathscr{T}) \oplus V_2(\mathscr{T})) \oplus V_3(\mathscr{T}) = $ (N $\oplus$ N) $\oplus$ N $= $ N $\oplus$ N $= $ N.

Thus, in this case, $V_1(\mathscr{T}) \oplus (V_2(\mathscr{T}) \oplus V_3(\mathscr{T})) = (V_1(\mathscr{T}) \oplus V_2(\mathscr{T})) \oplus V_3(\mathscr{T})$.

Quisque ullamcorper placerat ipsum. Cras nibh. Morbi vel justo vitae lacus tincidunt ultrices. Lorem ipsum dolor sit amet, consectetuer adipiscing elit. In hac habitasse platea dictumst. Integer tempus convallis augue. Etiam facilisis. Nunc elementum fermentum wisi. Aenean placerat. Ut imperdiet, enim sed gravida sollicitudin, felis odio placerat quam, ac pulvinar elit purus eget enim. Nunc vitae tortor. Proin tempus nibh sit amet nisl. Vivamus quis tortor vitae risus porta vehicula.

E   Distributivity of ⊗ Over ⊕

The distributivity of binary operation ⊗ over ⊕ supporting status E.

⊗	E	X	F	P	N	U
E	E	E	E	E	E	E
X	E	X	X	X	X	X
F	E	X	F	F	F	F
P	E	X	F	U	N	U
N	E	X	F	N	N	N
U	E	X	F	U	N	U

$$V(\mathcal{T}_1) \otimes (V_1(\mathcal{T}_2) \oplus V_2(\mathcal{T}_2)) \succeq (V(\mathcal{T}_1) \otimes V_1(\mathcal{T}_2)) \oplus (V(\mathcal{T}_1) \otimes V_2(\mathcal{T}_2)).$$

Proof We will prove this property in the following cases.

(1) $V(\mathcal{T}_1)$ is E. According to the operation table of ⊗, $V(\mathcal{T}_1) \otimes (V_1(\mathcal{T}_2) \oplus V_2(\mathcal{T}_2)) = E$, $V(\mathcal{T}_1) \otimes V_1(\mathcal{T}_2) = E$, and $V(\mathcal{T}_1) \otimes V_2(\mathcal{T}_2) = E$. Thus, $V(\mathcal{T}_1) \otimes (V_1(\mathcal{T}_2) \oplus V_2(\mathcal{T}_2)) = (V(\mathcal{T}_1) \otimes V_1(\mathcal{T}_2)) \oplus (V(\mathcal{T}_1) \otimes V_2(\mathcal{T}_2))$.

(2) $V(\mathcal{T}_1)$ is not E, and $V_1(\mathcal{T}_2) \oplus V_2(\mathcal{T}_2)$ is E. According to the operation table of ⊗, $V(\mathcal{T}_1) \otimes (V_1(\mathcal{T}_2) \oplus V_2(\mathcal{T}_2)) = E$.

(a) If one of $V_1(\mathcal{T}_2)$ and $V_2(\mathcal{T}_2)$ is E, then according to the operation table of ⊗ and ⊕, $(V(\mathcal{T}_1) \otimes V_1(\mathcal{T}_2)) \oplus (V(\mathcal{T}_1) \otimes V_2(\mathcal{T}_2)) = E$. Thus, $V(\mathcal{T}_1) \otimes (V_1(\mathcal{T}_2) \oplus V_2(\mathcal{T}_2)) = (V(\mathcal{T}_1) \otimes V_1(\mathcal{T}_2)) \oplus (V(\mathcal{T}_1) \otimes V_2(\mathcal{T}_2)) = E$.

(b) If $V(\mathcal{T}_1) = X$, and both $V_1(\mathcal{T}_2)$ and $V_2(\mathcal{T}_2)$ are not E, then according to the operation table of ⊗, $V(\mathcal{T}_1) \otimes V_1(\mathcal{T}_2) = X$, and $V(\mathcal{T}_1) \otimes V_2(\mathcal{T}_2) = X$. According to the operation table of ⊕, $(V(\mathcal{T}_1) \otimes V_1(\mathcal{T}_2)) \oplus (V(\mathcal{T}_1) \otimes V_2(\mathcal{T}_2)) = X$. Thus, $V(\mathcal{T}_1) \otimes (V_1(\mathcal{T}_2) \oplus V_2(\mathcal{T}_2)) \succ (V(\mathcal{T}_1) \otimes V_1(\mathcal{T}_2)) \oplus (V(\mathcal{T}_1) \otimes V_2(\mathcal{T}_2))$.

(c) If $V(\mathcal{T}_1)$ is not X, one of $V_1(\mathcal{T}_2)$ and $V_2(\mathcal{T}_2)$ is X, then the other one is F, P, N, or U. Without loss of generality, suppose that $V_1(\mathcal{T}_2) = X$, according to the operation table of ⊗, $V(\mathcal{T}_1) \otimes V_1(\mathcal{T}_2) = X$, and $V(\mathcal{T}_1) \otimes V_2(\mathcal{T}_2)$ can be F, N, or U. According to the operation table of ⊕, $(V(\mathcal{T}_1) \otimes V_1(\mathcal{T}_2)) \oplus (V(\mathcal{T}_1) \otimes V_2(\mathcal{T}_2)) = E$. Thus, $V(\mathcal{T}_1) \otimes (V_1(\mathcal{T}_2) \oplus V_2(\mathcal{T}_2)) = (V(\mathcal{T}_1) \otimes V_1(\mathcal{T}_2)) \oplus (V(\mathcal{T}_1) \otimes V_2(\mathcal{T}_2)) = E$.

(d) If $V(\mathcal{T}_1) = F$, both $V_1(\mathcal{T}_2)$ and $V_2(\mathcal{T}_2)$ are not E and X. According to the operation table of ⊗, $V(\mathcal{T}_1) \otimes V_1(\mathcal{T}_2) = F$, and $V(\mathcal{T}_1) \otimes V_2(\mathcal{T}_2) = F$. According to the operation table of ⊕, $(V(\mathcal{T}_1) \otimes V_1(\mathcal{T}_2)) \oplus (V(\mathcal{T}_1) \otimes V_2(\mathcal{T}_2)) = F$. Thus, $V(\mathcal{T}_1) \otimes (V_1(\mathcal{T}_2) \oplus V_2(\mathcal{T}_2)) \succ (V(\mathcal{T}_1) \otimes V_1(\mathcal{T}_2)) \oplus (V(\mathcal{T}_1) \otimes V_2(\mathcal{T}_2))$.

(e) If $V(\mathcal{T}_1)$ is not X and F, one of $V_1(\mathcal{T}_2)$ and $V_2(\mathcal{T}_2)$ is F, then the other one is P. Without loss of generality, suppose that $V_1(\mathcal{T}_2) = F$ and $V_2(\mathcal{T}_2) = P$, according to the operation table of ⊗, $V(\mathcal{T}_1) \otimes V_1(\mathcal{T}_2) = F$, and $V(\mathcal{T}_1) \otimes V_2(\mathcal{T}_2)$ can be N or U. According to the operation table of ⊕, $(V(\mathcal{T}_1) \otimes V_1(\mathcal{T}_2)) \oplus (V(\mathcal{T}_1) \otimes V_2(\mathcal{T}_2)) = F$. Thus, $V(\mathcal{T}_1) \otimes (V_1(\mathcal{T}_2) \oplus V_2(\mathcal{T}_2)) \succ (V(\mathcal{T}_1) \otimes V_1(\mathcal{T}_2)) \oplus (V(\mathcal{T}_1) \otimes V_2(\mathcal{T}_2))$.

(3) $V(\mathcal{T}_1)$ is X, and $V_1(\mathcal{T}_2) \oplus V_2(\mathcal{T}_2)$ is not E. According to the operation table of ⊗, $V(\mathcal{T}_1) \otimes (V_1(\mathcal{T}_2) \oplus V_2(\mathcal{T}_2)) = X$, $V(\mathcal{T}_1) \otimes V_1(\mathcal{T}_2) = X$ and $V(\mathcal{T}_1) \otimes V_2(\mathcal{T}_2) = X$. According to the operation table of ⊕, $(V(\mathcal{T}_1) \otimes V_1(\mathcal{T}_2)) \oplus (V(\mathcal{T}_1) \otimes V_2(\mathcal{T}_2)) = X$. Thus, $V(\mathcal{T}_1) \otimes (V_1(\mathcal{T}_2) \oplus V_2(\mathcal{T}_2)) = (V(\mathcal{T}_1) \otimes V_1(\mathcal{T}_2)) \oplus (V(\mathcal{T}_1) \otimes V_2(\mathcal{T}_2)) = X$.

(4) $V(\mathcal{T}_1)$ is not E, and $V_1(\mathcal{T}_2) \oplus V_2(\mathcal{T}_2) = $ X. According to the operation table of $\otimes$, $V(\mathcal{T}_1) \otimes (V_1(\mathcal{T}_2) \oplus V_2(\mathcal{T}_2)) = $ X. Since $V_1(\mathcal{T}_2) \oplus V_2(\mathcal{T}_2) = $ X, both $V_1(\mathcal{T}_2)$ and $V_2(\mathcal{T}_2)$ are X. According to the operation table of $\otimes$, $V(\mathcal{T}_1) \otimes V_1(\mathcal{T}_2) = $ X and $V(\mathcal{T}_1) \otimes V_2(\mathcal{T}_2) = $ X. According to the operation table of $\oplus$, $(V(\mathcal{T}_1) \otimes V_1(\mathcal{T}_2)) \oplus (V(\mathcal{T}_1) \otimes V_2(\mathcal{T}_2)) = $ X. Thus, $V(\mathcal{T}_1) \otimes (V_1(\mathcal{T}_2) \oplus V_2(\mathcal{T}_2)) = (V(\mathcal{T}_1) \otimes V_1(\mathcal{T}_2)) \oplus (V(\mathcal{T}_1) \otimes V_2(\mathcal{T}_2)) = $ X.

(5) $V(\mathcal{T}_1)$ is F, and $V_1(\mathcal{T}_2) \oplus V_2(\mathcal{T}_2)$ is not E and X. According to the operation table of $\otimes$, $V(\mathcal{T}_1) \otimes (V_1(\mathcal{T}_2) \oplus V_2(\mathcal{T}_2)) = $ F, $V(\mathcal{T}_1) \otimes V_1(\mathcal{T}_2) = $ F and $V(\mathcal{T}_1) \otimes V_2(\mathcal{T}_2) = $ F. According to the operation table of $\oplus$, $(V(\mathcal{T}_1) \otimes V_1(\mathcal{T}_2)) \oplus (V(\mathcal{T}_1) \otimes V_2(\mathcal{T}_2)) = $ F. Thus, $V(\mathcal{T}_1) \otimes (V_1(\mathcal{T}_2) \oplus V_2(\mathcal{T}_2)) = (V(\mathcal{T}_1) \otimes V_1(\mathcal{T}_2)) \oplus (V(\mathcal{T}_1) \otimes V_2(\mathcal{T}_2)) = $ F.

(6) $V(\mathcal{T}_1)$ is not E and X, and $V_1(\mathcal{T}_2) \oplus V_2(\mathcal{T}_2)$ is F. According to the operation table of $\otimes$, $V(\mathcal{T}_1) \otimes (V_1(\mathcal{T}_2) \oplus V_2(\mathcal{T}_2)) = $ F. Since $V_1(\mathcal{T}_2) \oplus V_2(\mathcal{T}_2) = $ F, at least one of $V_1(\mathcal{T}_2)$ and $V_2(\mathcal{T}_2)$ is F. Without loss of generality, suppose that $V_1(\mathcal{T}_2) = $ F, then according to the operation table of $\otimes$, $V(\mathcal{T}_1) \otimes V_1(\mathcal{T}_2) = $ F and $V(\mathcal{T}_1) \otimes V_2(\mathcal{T}_2)$ can only be F, N, and U. According to the operation table of $\oplus$, $(V(\mathcal{T}_1) \otimes V_1(\mathcal{T}_2)) \oplus (V(\mathcal{T}_1) \otimes V_2(\mathcal{T}_2)) = $ F. Thus, $V(\mathcal{T}_1) \otimes (V_1(\mathcal{T}_2) \oplus V_2(\mathcal{T}_2)) = (V(\mathcal{T}_1) \otimes V_1(\mathcal{T}_2)) \oplus (V(\mathcal{T}_1) \otimes V_2(\mathcal{T}_2)) = $ F.

(7) $V(\mathcal{T}_1)$ is N, and $V_1(\mathcal{T}_2) \oplus V_2(\mathcal{T}_2)$ is not E, X and F. According to the operation table of $\otimes$, $V(\mathcal{T}_1) \otimes (V_1(\mathcal{T}_2) \oplus V_2(\mathcal{T}_2)) = $ N, $V(\mathcal{T}_1) \otimes V_1(\mathcal{T}_2) = $ N, and $V(\mathcal{T}_1) \otimes V_2(\mathcal{T}_2) = $ N. According to the operation table of $\oplus$, $(V(\mathcal{T}_1) \otimes V_1(\mathcal{T}_2)) \oplus (V(\mathcal{T}_1) \otimes V_2(\mathcal{T}_2)) = $ N. Thus, $V(\mathcal{T}_1) \otimes (V_1(\mathcal{T}_2) \oplus V_2(\mathcal{T}_2)) = (V(\mathcal{T}_1) \otimes V_1(\mathcal{T}_2)) \oplus (V(\mathcal{T}_1) \otimes V_2(\mathcal{T}_2)) = $ N.

(8) $V(\mathcal{T}_1)$ is not E, X, and F, and $V_1(\mathcal{T}_2) \oplus V_2(\mathcal{T}_2)$ is N. According to the operation table of $\otimes$, $V(\mathcal{T}_1) \otimes (V_1(\mathcal{T}_2) \oplus V_2(\mathcal{T}_2)) = $ N. Since $V_1(\mathcal{T}_2) \oplus V_2(\mathcal{T}_2) = $ N, both $V_1(\mathcal{T}_2)$ and $V_2(\mathcal{T}_2)$ are N. According to the operation table of $\oplus$, $(V(\mathcal{T}_1) \otimes V_1(\mathcal{T}_2)) \oplus (V(\mathcal{T}_1) \otimes V_2(\mathcal{T}_2)) = $ N. Thus, $V(\mathcal{T}_1) \otimes (V_1(\mathcal{T}_2) \oplus V_2(\mathcal{T}_2)) = (V(\mathcal{T}_1) \otimes V_1(\mathcal{T}_2)) \oplus (V(\mathcal{T}_1) \otimes V_2(\mathcal{T}_2)) = $ N.

(9) $V(\mathcal{T}_1)$ is P or U, and $V_1(\mathcal{T}_2) \oplus V_2(\mathcal{T}_2)$ is not E, X, F, and N. According to the operation table of $\otimes$, $V(\mathcal{T}_1) \otimes (V_1(\mathcal{T}_2) \oplus V_2(\mathcal{T}_2)) = $ U. Since $V_1(\mathcal{T}_2) \oplus V_2(\mathcal{T}_2)$ is not E, X, F, and N, $V_1(\mathcal{T}_2)$ and $V_2(\mathcal{T}_2)$ can only be P, N, or U, and at most one of them is N. According to the operation table of $\otimes$, $V(\mathcal{T}_1) \otimes V_1(\mathcal{T}_2)$ and $V(\mathcal{T}_1) \otimes V_2(\mathcal{T}_2)$ can only be N or U, and at most one of them is N. According to the operation table of $\oplus$, $(V(\mathcal{T}_1) \otimes V_1(\mathcal{T}_2)) \oplus (V(\mathcal{T}_1) \otimes V_2(\mathcal{T}_2)) = $ U. Thus, $V(\mathcal{T}_1) \otimes (V_1(\mathcal{T}_2) \oplus V_2(\mathcal{T}_2)) = (V(\mathcal{T}_1) \otimes V_1(\mathcal{T}_2)) \oplus (V(\mathcal{T}_1) \otimes V_2(\mathcal{T}_2)) = $ U.

(10) $V(\mathcal{T}_1)$ is not E, X, F, and N, and $V_1(\mathcal{T}_2) \oplus V_2(\mathcal{T}_2)$ is P or U. According to the operation table of $\otimes$, $V(\mathcal{T}_1) \otimes (V_1(\mathcal{T}_2) \oplus V_2(\mathcal{T}_2)) = $ U. Since $V_1(\mathcal{T}_2) \oplus V_2(\mathcal{T}_2)$ is P or U, $V_1(\mathcal{T}_2)$ and $V_2(\mathcal{T}_2)$ can only be P, N, or U, and at most one of them is N. According to the operation table of $\otimes$, $V(\mathcal{T}_1) \otimes V_1(\mathcal{T}_2)$ and $V(\mathcal{T}_1) \otimes V_2(\mathcal{T}_2)$ can only be N or U, and at most one of them is N. According to the operation table of $\oplus$, $(V(\mathcal{T}_1) \otimes V_1(\mathcal{T}_2)) \oplus (V(\mathcal{T}_1) \otimes V_2(\mathcal{T}_2)) = $ U. Thus, $V(\mathcal{T}_1) \otimes (V_1(\mathcal{T}_2) \oplus V_2(\mathcal{T}_2)) = (V(\mathcal{T}_1) \otimes V_1(\mathcal{T}_2)) \oplus (V(\mathcal{T}_1) \otimes V_2(\mathcal{T}_2)) = $ U.

Quisque ullamcorper placerat ipsum. Cras nibh. Morbi vel justo vitae lacus tincidunt ultrices. Lorem ipsum dolor sit amet, consectetuer adipiscing elit. In hac habitasse platea dictumst. Integer tempus convallis augue. Etiam facilisis. Nunc elementum fermentum wisi. Aenean placerat. Ut imperdiet, enim sed gravida sollicitudin, felis odio placerat quam, ac pulvinar elit purus eget enim. Nunc vitae tortor. Proin tempus nibh sit amet nisl. Vivamus quis tortor vitae risus porta vehicula.

Reference

1. W.-T. Tsai, C. Colbourn, J. Luo, G. Qi, Q. Li, X. Bai, Test algebra for combinatorial testing, in *Proceedings of the 2013 8th International Workshop on Automation of Software Test (AST)* (May 2013), pp. 19–25

Chapter 5
Concurrent Test Algebra Execution with Combinatorial Testing

Abstract Software-as-a-Service (SaaS) application plays an important role in daily life and needs to have high reliability and availability before publishing. Testing SaaS applications become important, as the large number of testing prior to their deployment. TA identifies faults in combinatorial testing for SaaS applications using existing test results and eliminates those related faults. Although TA eliminates a large number of configurations from considerations, it is still difficult to finish testing enormous combinations of services in a reasonable time. To improve TA analysis, this chapter proposes a concurrent TA analysis. It allocates workloads into different clusters of computers and performs TA analysis from 2-way to 6-way configurations. Different database designs are used to store the test results of various configurations. Faulty and operational table search algorithms are proposed to retrieve existing test results. One 25-component experiment is simulated using the proposed solutions. The same experiment is also simulated on multiple processors for concurrent TA analysis.

5.1 TA Analysis Framework

Figure 5.1 shows the relationship between TA and combinatorial testing. Combinatorial testing can use AETG, AR, or IPO [1] to identify P and F configurations, and even fault locations. The identified configurations and fault locations are saved as test results for future use. TA automatically detects X or F configurations using existing X or F results. All X and F configurations are eliminated from testing considerations. In combinatorial testing, test workloads of those X and F candidate configurations are reduced by TA analysis. Similarly, those N configurations can also be eliminated from considerations.

Figure 5.2 shows the concurrent design for TA analysis [3]. There are many candidate components for tenants to pick up to compose their own applications. The composed applications of different tenants will be assigned to different clusters for analysis. Each cluster has multiple servers to handle TA tasks in parallel.

Parts of this chapter is reprinted from [3], with permission from IEEE.

© The Author(s) 2017
W. Tsai and G. Qi, *Combinatorial Testing in Cloud Computing*,
SpringerBriefs in Computer Science, https://doi.org/10.1007/978-981-10-4481-6_5

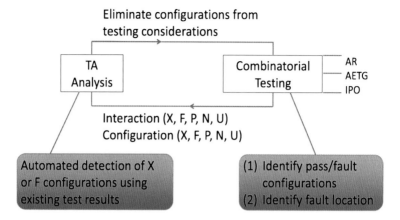

Fig. 5.1 The relationship between TA and combinatorial testing

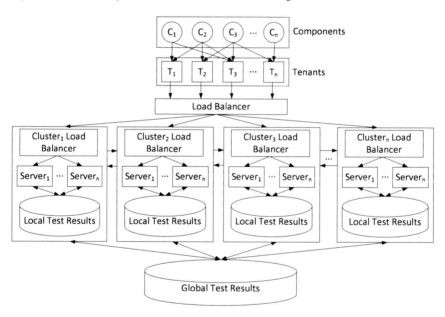

Fig. 5.2 Concurrent TA analysis design

The two-level architecture not only automatically balances the workloads across multiple clusters and servers but also scales up with increasing loads with automated expansion. This is similar to the scalability architecture commonly used in SaaS [2].

- Allocate by tenants at the first level: The tenants will be clustered based on the similarity measured by configurations. Two tenants are similar to each other if two share many components. Similar tenants are grouped and assigned to the same cluster.
- Allocate by configurations at second level: The configurations of each tenant assigned to one cluster will be assigned to the same or different server in each cluster for analyzing.

Concurrent algorithm shown in Algorithm 3 is proposed to solve the distribution and collection of testing workloads.

Algorithm 3 Concurrent for TA Analysis

Input:
    Candidate test configuration c_i, map cluster p_i,
Output:
    Reduce testing result r_i, testing result of test case tr_i,
1: $p_i = (\text{id } n, \sum c_i$ of one candidate test set)
2: **for** all p_i **do**
3:     return tr_i
4: **end for**
5: $r_i = (n, \sum c_i, tr_i)$
6: **for** all p_i **do**
7:     return r_i
8: **end for**

The high-level load balancer allocates testing and TA analysis tasks to different clusters, and each cluster has its own local load balancer and it will dispatch testing and TA analysis tasks to different servers within the cluster. All clusters share a global database, and each sever within a cluster shares a local database for efficient processing.

Test scripts and databases can be stored at the global database as well as at local databases within clusters. As TA rules automatically detect test result consistency, thus, any temporary inconsistency between local database with the global database can be resolved quickly once communicated.

The finished test results will be saved as PTR (Previous Test Result) and shared. Before saving, all test results must be verified by the test oracle to check the correctness. Only the correct test results will be saved in test database. Same configurations may be analyzed in different clusters. In this case, if one cluster gets test result of any configuration first, it can be shared and reused by others. For example, $cluster_1$ gets that configuration (a, b) fails in combinatorial testing first. $cluster_2$ and $cluster_3$ can reuse the shared faulty result of configuration (a, b).

The following example illustrates the testing process of fifteen configurations. All feasible configurations should be tested. For simplicity, assume that only configuration (c, d, f) is faulty, and only configuration (c, d, e) is infeasible, and all other configurations are operational. The existing test results of configurations can be used to analyze test results of candidate configurations for reducing test workloads.

Example 1: If one assigns 1–10 configurations into $Server_1$, 6–15 configurations into $Server_2$, and 1–5, 11–15 configurations into $Server_3$.

	$Server_1$	$Server_2$	$Server_3$	$Merged\ Results$
(a,b,c,d)	P		P	P
(a,b,c,e)	P		P	P
(a,b,c,f)	P		P	P
(a,b,d,e)	P		P	P
(a,b,d,f)	P		P	P
(a,b,e,f)	P	P		P
(a,c,d,e)	X	X		X
(a,c,d,f)	F	F		F
(a,c,e,f)	P	P		P
(a,d,e,f)	P	P		P
(b,c,d,e)		X	X	X
(b,c,d,f)		F	F	F
(b,c,e,f)		P	P	P
(b,d,e,f)		P	P	P
(c,d,e,f)		X	X	X

Example 2: If one assigns configurations 1, 3, 5, 7, 9, 11, 13, 15 into $Server_1$, configurations 2, 4, 6, 8, 10, 12, 14 into $Server_2$, and 4–11 configurations into $Server_3$. If $Server_1$ and $Server_3$ do their own testing first, $Server_2$ can reuse test results of interactions from them to eliminate interactions that need to be tested. For example, when testing 2-way interactions of configuration (b, c, d, f) in $Server_2$, it can reuse the test results of (b, c), (b, d) of configuration (b, c, d, e) from $Server_3$, (b, f) of configuration (a, b, c, f) from $Server_1$. They are all passed, and it can reuse the test results of (b, c, d) of configuration (a, b, c, d) from $Server_1$, (b, c, f) of configuration (a, b, c, f) from $Server_1$, (b, d, f) of configuration (a, b, d, f) from $Server_1$, and (c, d, f) of configuration (a, c, d, f) from $Server_3$. Because (c, d, f) is faulty, it can deduce that 4-way configuration (b, c, d, f) is also faulty. For the sets of configuration that are overlapping, their returned test results from different servers are the same. The merged results of these results also stay the same.

	$Server_1$	$Server_2$	$Server_3$	$Merged\ Results$
(a,b,c,d)	P			P
(a,b,c,e)		P		P
(a,b,c,f)	P			P
(a,b,d,e)		P	P	P
(a,b,d,f)	P		P	P
(a,b,e,f)		P	P	P
(a,c,d,e)	X		X	X
(a,c,d,f)		F	F	F
(a,c,e,f)	P		P	P
(a,d,e,f)		P	P	P
(b,c,d,e)	X		X	X
(b,c,d,f)		F		F
(b,c,e,f)	P			P
(b,d,e,f)		P		P
(c,d,e,f)	X			X

If $Server_1$ and $Server_3$ do their own testing first, $Server_2$ can reuse test results of interactions from them to eliminate interactions that need to be tested. For example, when testing 2-way interactions of configuration (b, c, d, f) in $Server_2$, it can reuse the test results of (b, c), (b, d) of configuration (b, c, d, e) from $Server_3$, (b, f) of configuration (a, b, c, f) from $Server_1$. They are all passed, and it can reuse the test results of (b, c, d) of configuration (a, b, c, d) from $Server_1$, (b, c, f) of configuration (a, b, c, f) from $Server_1$, (b, d, f) of configuration (a, b, d, f) from $Server_1$, and (c, d, f) of configuration (a, c, d, f) from $Server_3$. Because (c, d, f) is faulty, it can deduce that 4-way interaction (b, c, d, f) is also faulty. For the sets of configuration that are overlapping, their returned test results from different servers are the same. The merged results of these results also stay the same.

The returned merged results from these two examples are same. Analyzing the returned results, it can get the following results:

- **All 2-way interactions**: All of them pass the testing.
- **All 3-way interactions**: Except interaction (c, d, e) and (c, d, f), all the left 3-way interactions pass the testing.
- **All 4-ways interactions**: The 4-way interactions that contain (c, d, e) and (c, d, f), such as (a, c, d, e), (a, c, d, f), (b, c, d, e), (b, c, d, f), and (c, d, e, f), do not pass the testing. All the left 4-way interactions pass the testing.
- **All fifteen configurations**: Configurations (a, c, d, e), (a, c, d, f), (b, c, d, e), (b, c, d, f), and (c, d, e, f) do not pass the testing. All the left configurations pass the testing.

5.1.1 The Role of N in Concurrent Combinatorial Testing

Not only interactions, sets of configurations, CS_1, CS_2, ..., CS_K can be allocated to different processors (or clusters) for testing, and the test results can then be merged. The sets can be non-overlapping or overlapping, and the merge process can be arbitrary. For example, say the result of CS_i is RCS_i, the merge process can be $(\cdots((((RCS_1 + RCS_2) + RCS_3) + RCS_4) + \cdots + RCS_K)$, or $(\cdots((((RCS_K + RCS_{k-1}) + RCS_{k-2}) + \cdots + RCS_1)$, or any other sequence that includes all RCS_i, for $i = 1$ to K. This is true because RCS is simply a set of $V(\mathcal{T}_j)$ for any interaction $\mathcal{T}_j$ in the configuration CS_i. If an algorithm such as AR is used, any P results reduce the number of tests needed for t-way interaction testing. Any F result in TA is useful to use 2-way, 3-way, and $(t - 1)$-way interaction testing results to reduce testing effort for t-way interaction testing. Thus, both P and F results are useful in reducing testing effort. The N results are also useful, and any configuration that is marked as N means that it is not necessary to perform testing, and this can reduce the number of configurations and interactions to test. This is particularly useful when the number of configurations is large, as the set of configurations can be divided into different (not necessarily non-overlapping) sets, one for each server or cluster of servers. In this way, any N results help in divide-and-conquer approach to address large combinatorial testing. For example, if a SaaS system has $1M$ tenant applications, but the SaaS platform has over $10,000$ processors, then each processor needs to handle only $\frac{1M}{10K} = 100$ tenant applications. Each server can divide this testing process again, performing testing 10 times, each testing 10 tenants with test results stored in the database. In this way, large-scale combinatorial testing can be performed.

5.1.2 Modified Testing Process

Perform 2-way interaction testing first. Before going on to 3-way interaction testing, use the results of 2-way testing to eliminate cases. The testing process stops when finishing testing all t-way interactions. The analysis of t-way interactions is based on the PTRs of all $(t - i)$-way interactions for $1 \le i < t$. The superset of infeasible, irrelevant, and faulty test cases do not need to be tested. The test results of the superset can be obtained by TA operations and must be infeasible, irrelevant, or faulty. But the superset of test cases with unknown indicator must be tested. In this way, a large repeating testing workload can be reduced.

For n components, all t-way interactions for $t \ge 2$ are composed by 2-way, 3-way, ..., t-way interactions. In n components combinatorial testing, the number of 2-way interactions is equal to C_2^n. In general, the number of t-way interactions is equal to C_t^n. More interactions are treated when $C_t^n > C_{t-1}^n$, which happens when $t \le \frac{n}{2}$. The total number of interactions examined is $\sum_{i=2}^t C_i^n$.

5.2 TA Analysis Algorithm

For new candidate testing configurations, the testing process as follows:

1. **Search in F-table**
   For n-way candidate configuration, search in related F-table from 2-way to n-way
   to check whether it contains any F interactions. If yes, candidate configuration
   is faulty and can be eliminated from testing. Otherwise, search in P-table to find
   which test results can be reused.

   - *Best condition*: For a n-way candidate configuration, related 2-way faulty
     interaction is found in F-table. Stop searching in F-table and return F as the
     test result of candidate configuration.
   - *Worst condition*: All related interactions of n-way candidate configuration
     are searched in F-table, but none is found in F-table. The n-way candidate
     configuration cannot be eliminated from the TA analysis.

2. **Search in P-table** For n-way candidate configuration, search all its related interactions from n-way to 2-way interaction P-table. All found interactions can be
   excluded from the candidate testing list. Only those missing interactions need to
   be tested.

   - *Best condition*: For an n-way candidate configuration, all related interactions
     are found in P-table, thus the configuration is operational.
   - *Worst condition*: Any related interactions cannot be found in P-table, and thus
     related interactions need to be tested.

Algorithm 4 F-table Search Algorithm

Input:
   F-table, n-way candidate configuration ($n \leq 6$)
Output:
   Test results of candidate configuration
1: Calculate all related interactions of n-way candidate configurations
2: Search related interactions from 2-way to n-way interaction F-table
3: **for** (i=2; i<=n; ++) **do**
4:    Traverse i-way's F-table to search related interactions
5:    **if** any interactions are found **then**
6:       Return faulty result
7:       Stop
8:    **end if**
9: **end for**

   Example 1: Search configuration (a,b,d,f). Search the related interaction of configuration (a,b,d,f) in F-table. Find interaction (d,f) is faulty. So $V(a, b, d, f) = F$.
   Example 2: Search configuration (a,b,e,f). Search the related interactions of configuration (a,b,e,f) in F-table. No one can be found. Then, search all related interactions in P-table. 3-way interaction (a,b,e), (a,b,f), and (b,e,f) are found in 3-way

---

Algorithm 5 Configuration P-table Search Algorithm

Input:
   P-table, n-way candidate configuration ($n \leq 6$)
Output:
   Non-found interaction
1: Calculate all related interactions of n-way candidate configuration from n-way to 2-way
2: Put all related interactions into different lists according to component number
3: Search interactions from n-way to 2-way interaction P-table
4: **for** (i=n; i<2; −−) **do**
5:    Traverse i-ways P-table to search for i-way interaction of candidate configuration
6:    **if** any interactions are found **then**
7:       Delete the found interactions from the list
8:       **if** the list is empty **then**
9:          Return empty list
10:          Stop
11:       **end if**
12:    **end if**
13:    Return list
14: **end for**

P-table. As TA proved, $V(a, b, e, f) = V(a, b, e) \otimes V(a, b, f) = V(a, b, e) \otimes V(b, e, f) = V(a, b, f) \otimes V(b, e, f)$. Since all 3-way interactions of (a,b,e,f) can be found in P-table, there is no need to search and test all its 2-way interactions. All 2-way interactions are operational. Only interaction (a,b,e,f) is not covered. So the testing workloads of configuration (a,b,e,f) are reduced to test interaction (a,b,e,f) only to finalize the test result of configuration (a,b,e,f).

5.3 TA Analysis Process and Related Considerations

5.3.1 Analysis Process

1. 2-way TA analysis:

   a. Use proposed search algorithms and distribute candidate configurations into different processors for execution. Different distribution methods can be used, such as based on the similarity among different configurations, the usage of different configurations, or the mixed methods;

   b. Use P_2 (P table for 2-way interactions) to reduce testing effort. A P_2 configuration will not be N, and will not be X_2 (X table for 2-way interactions), but maybe X_3 (X table for 3-way interactions).

   c. Complete testing all 2-way configurations (thus, some N configurations may be around), and store all the results at P_2, F_2, N_2, and X_3 tables.

2. 3-way TA analysis using 2-way data:

    a. Eliminate those 3-ways configurations that have X_2, F_2, and N_2 2-way configurations. Those 3-ways interactions are sent to X_3, F_3, N_3 tables.

    b. Divide the P_2 configurations into different sets of configurations and send to different processors for analyzing.

    c. Use P_2 (2-way P interaction) to reduce testing effort.

    d. Complete testing all feasible 3-way configurations.

3. 4-way TA analysis using 2-way and 3-way data:

    a. Eliminate those 4-ways configurations that have X_2, F_2, and N_2 2-way configurations, and X_3, F_3, and N_3 3-way configurations. Those 4-ways interactions are sent to X_4, F_4, N_4 tables.

    b. Divide the P_2 and P_3 configurations into different sets of configurations and send to different processors for analyzing.

    c. Use P_2 and P_3 (3-way P interaction) to reduce testing effort.

    d. Complete testing all feasible 4-way configurations.

The above steps can be repeated for 5-way and 6-way TA analysis.

5.3.2 Adjustment in Analyzing

All the possible configurations can be divided into different sets for different processors for analyzing. For simplicity, it is better to assign a set of related configurations to the same server. If X and F configurations are found, the related configurations can be easily eliminated in one server. There is no need to coordinate the results among different servers. Otherwise, the coordination cost is high. For example, set_1 is allocated to $processor_1$ for analysis. $processor_1$ will select configurations or tenant applications in set_1 for analyzing, If everything is great, i.e., all P, the test results are great, the analyzing process can stop. Otherwise, it requires further testing.

Lots of bugs exist in the candidate interactions. It is different to know the distributions of bugs. The bugs may not be evenly assign to different servers. Stop testing if the fault rate is high. The F test results can be used to deduce other F interactions by TA saving significant effort.

Multiple ways allocate configurations to processors, such as:

- **Tenant membership**: Configurations of one tenant application are assigned to one server as much as possible. It reduces the coordination costs of configuration test results among different servers.
- **Functionality information**: Tenant applications, that implement the same or similar functions, often share same and closely related configurations. Clustering these tenant applications based on functionality also increases the test efficiency.

- **Random**: Randomly assign candidate configurations to different clusters. Load balancing may not be considered in assigning process and some configurations may be tested by multiple processors for redundant testing.
- P/F **configuration allocation**: Allocate P/F configurations to processors at local cache. Each processor can use the assigned P/F configurations to analyze candidate configurations.

5.4   Test Database Design

5.4.1   X *and* F *Table Design*

When one X or F interaction is saved in databases, test results of related configurations can be deduced. The saved test results are shared to all servers.

The test results tables correspond to the n-way interactions that have their own tables. If too many results are saved in one table, the table will be split for efficiency. The usage of each interaction decides the storage position of test result. The test results of frequently used interactions are saved in the top of data table.

5.4.2   P *Table Design*

Different from X and F interactions, the P test results can be reused to reduce test workloads and increase the testing efficiency, but they cannot eliminate the untested configurations from testing considerations. The P-table can follow the same design as X-table and F-table such as placing high priority items on the top, and priority can be adjusted dynamically. The usage ranking mechanism and data migration rules can also be used. The difference is that all P interactions must be saved in corresponding data table.

However, TA operation rules for P are different from operation rules for X or F. Specifically, the n-way ($n \geq 3$) configurations contain 2-way interactions. For any operational n-way ($n \geq 3$) configurations, all their sub-interactions (2-way interactions) must be operational.

Unlike X-table or F-table, P-table stores all P interactions without any omitting. So another difference is that relationships exist and can be traced among different n-way interaction table. For example, $(a, b, c) \succ (a, b)(b, c)$ or $(a, c)(b, c)$. If $(a, b, c) = P$, (a, b), (a, c), and (b, c) in 2-way interaction table have connections with (a, b, c) in 3-way interaction table.

A $(n+1)$-way configuration contains n-way configurations. The existing test results of n-way configurations can be used to reduce the testing workloads of (n-1)-way configuration. In this paper, TA build 2-way P-table first, then 3-way, 4-way, 5-way, until 6-way.

Testing n-way configuration includes testing all its sub-configurations and itself. For candidate n-way configuration, TA searches existing test results from n-way to 2-way P-table. If n-way interaction of candidate configuration can be found in n-way P-table, stop searching and use the found operational result. Otherwise, search (n-1)-way P-table to find all existing test results of its sub-interactions. If all its (n-1)-way interactions are found in P-table, stop searching and only n-way interaction itself needs to be tested to finalize its test result. If not, only the non-found interactions need to be tested. For non-found interactions, repeat the previous procedures from (n-2)-way to 2-way P-table.

The following two examples show the search process. Suppose configuration (a,b,c,d,e) has never been tested before.

- Configuration (a,b,c,d,e) has five 4-way sub-interactions (a,b,c,d), (a,b,c,e), (a,b, d,e), (a,c,d,e), and (b,c,d,e). If these five interactions are found in P-table, only interaction (a,b,c,d,e) itself needs to be tested to finalize the test result.
- If four of its 4-way sub-interactions (a,b,c,d), (a,b,c,e), (a,b,d,e), and (a,c,d,e) are found in P-table, only interaction (b,c,d,e) needs to be tested. Repeat the same process in searching sub-interaction of interaction (b,c,d,e) in P-table. The similar process will be repeated until all its saved sub-interactions are found in P-table. Only non-found sub-interactions and interaction (a,b,c,d,e) itself need to be tested to finalize the test result.

5.4.3   N *and* U *Table Design*

In these two tables, test results of saved interactions may be changed by testing or TA analysis. Except adding new results, the deletion of existing test results often happens in N-table and U-table. Decreasing the data movement costs needs to consider in data table design. When one of N or U interactions changes its status, the previous saved status is deleted and empty space is left in test database. It is not good to move saved data forward to fill the empty spaces immediately. The system allows test database has a ceratin number of empty spaces. When empty spaces reach the threshold, the system moves saved data forward to fill the empty space. There is a trade-off between system efficiency and data movement costs for choosing reasonable threshold.

5.5   Experiment

The authors have performed experimentation using simulation data and data from published eScience software. The authors are developing a SaaS using the published software in an eScience Web site (myexperiment.org) with software contributed by scientists worldwide. Each software with its components in the myexperiment.org can be treated as a tenant application, and a collection of software can be incorporated as a SaaS system.

Numerous simulations have been performed, and this section provides one example with 25 components, and each component has two options. The total number of test configurations is 2^{50} (approximately $1.13 * 10^{15}$). The experiments are done for t-way configurations for $2 \le t \le 6$. All simulations are run on Intel Core 2 Quad CPU 2.40GHz machine. The numbers of t-way configurations for this example are listed in Table 5.1.

The following three tables list the initial infeasible (Table 5.2), faulty (Table 5.3), and irrelevant (Table 5.4) configurations. Tables 5.2 and 5.3 also listed the related infeasible and faulty configuration after. For example, if (A, B) is infeasible, (A, B, C) and (A, B, D) are all infeasible. Other than infeasible, faulty, and irrelevant configurations, the rest of configurations is either operational or unknown.

The irrelevant configurations are stored in the N-table. The initial N-table contains:

TA is then used to identify those configurations that need to be tested by first eliminating those configurations that have been identified to be X, F, or N. Other

Table 5.1 The number of T-way configurations from 2-way to 6-way

Range	Size
2-way configurations	1,200
3-way configurations	18,400
4-way configurations	202,400
5-way configurations	1,700,160
6-way configurations	11,334,400
Configurations from 2-way to 6-way	13,256,560

Table 5.2 The initial setting ups of infeasible configurations

Range	Initial infeasible configuration size	Related infeasible configuration size
2-way configurations	10	10
3-way configurations	100	560
4-way configurations	1,000	15,520
5-way configurations	10,000	286,080
6-way configurations	100,000	3,280,400

Table 5.3 The initial setting ups of faulty configurations

Range	Initial faulty configuration size	Related faulty configuration size
2-way configurations	25	25
3-way configurations	8	1,158
4-way configurations	0	25,652
5-way configurations	0	361,592
6-way configurations	1	3,640,561

Table 5.4 The initial setting ups of irrelevant configurations

Range	Size
All 2-way configurations	20
All 3-way configurations	200
All 4-way configurations	2,000
All 5-way configurations	20,000
All 6-way configurations	200,000

Table 5.5 The different initial P-table settings

Range	Size					
Percentage	5%	10%	20%	30%	40%	50%
2-way configurations	57	115	229	344	458	573
3-way configurations	824	1,648	3,296	4,945	6,593	8,241
4-way configurations	7,961	15,923	31,846	47,768	63,691	79,614
5-way configurations	51,624	103,249	206,498	309,746	412,995	516,244
6-way configurations	210,672	421,344	842,688	1,264,032	1,685,376	2,106,720

Table 5.6 The different initial U-table settings

Range	Size					
Percentage	5%	10%	20%	30%	40%	50%
2-way configurations	1,088	1,030	916	801	687	572
3-way configurations	15,658	14,834	13,186	11,537	9,889	8,241
4-way configurations	151,267	143,305	127,382	111,460	95,539	79,614
5-way configurations	980,864	929,239	825,990	722,742	619,493	516,244
6-way configurations	4,002,767	3,792,095	3,370,751	2,949,407	2,528,063	2,106,719

than infeasible, faulty, and irrelevant configurations, the candidate configurations are operational or unknown. The following attempts change the ratio of initial operational and unknown configurations to find the relationship between initial P-table and TA efficiency.

Tables 5.5 and 5.6 show the input to the simulation with different percentages of configurations, specifically 5, 10, 20, 30, 40, and 50% of configurations have status of P (operational) in Tables 5.5 and 5.6 show the corresponding data for U (unknown) configurations from 5 to 50% of initial configurations are operational (P).

Table 5.7 and Fig. 5.3 show the results of simulation, the data demonstrated that consistently the TA has eliminated 97.982% of configurations from testing consideration.

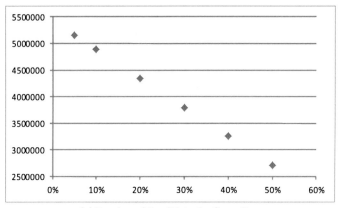

(a) Number of Candidate Configurations

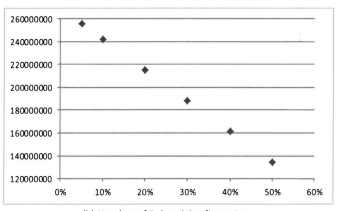

(b) Number of Related Configurations

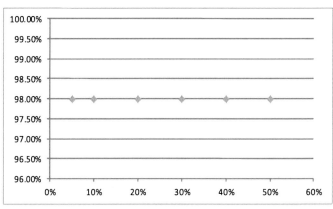

(c) Percentage of Reduced Workloads

Fig. 5.3 The simulation results

Table 5.7 The related and reduced configurations with different settings

	5%	10%	20%	30%	40%	50%
Involved Configurations (a)	$2.55*10^8$	$2.41*10^8$	$2.15*10^8$	$1.88*10^8$	$1.61*10^8$	$1.34*10^8$
Reduced Configurations (b)	$2.50*10^8$	$2.37*10^8$	$2.11*10^8$	$1.84*10^8$	$1.58*10^8$	$1.32*10^8$
Configurations to be tested (c)	$5.15*10^6$	$4.88*10^6$	$4.34*10^6$	$3.80*10^6$	$3.25*10^6$	$2.71*10^6$
Reduced Workloads Percentage (b/a)	97.982%	97.982%	97.982%	97.982%	97.982%	97.982%

5.6 Conclusion

This chapter proposes TA analysis framework to identify faults and eliminate related candidate-faults in SaaS combinatorial testing by using existing test results. The testing analysis process and related search algorithms are discussed. The specific test database is designed for each status in TA analysis. A 25-component experiment is simulated concurrently by TA analysis. The experiment results show that 97.982% of involved configurations are eliminated from testing considerations by TA analysis.

References

1. A. Calvagna, A. Gargantini. IPO-s: incremental generation of combinatorial interaction test data based on symmetries of covering arrays., in *Proceedings of the International Conference on Software Testing, Verification and Validation Workshops, 2009. ICSTW '09* (2009), pp. 10–18. doi:10.1109/ICSTW.2009.7
2. W.-T. Tsai, Y. Huang, X. Bai, J. Gao, Scalable architecture for SaaS, in *Proceedings of 15th IEEE International Symposium on Object Component Service-oriented Real-time Distributed Computing (ISORC '12)* (Apr 2012)
3. W.-T. Tsai, J. Luo, G. Qi, W. Wu. Concurrent test algebra execution with combinatorial testing, in *Proceedings of 8th IEEE International Symposium on Service-Oriented System Engineering (SOSE2014)* (2014)

Chapter 6
Test Algebra Execution in a Cloud Environment

Abstract Testing SaaS applications are challenging, because a large number of configurations need to be tested. Faulty configurations should be identified and corrected before the delivery of SaaS applications. TA proposes an effective way to reuse existing test results to identify test results of candidate configurations, and it also defines rules to permit results to be combined, and to identify the faulty interactions. Using the TA, configurations can be tested concurrently on different servers and in any order. This chapter proposes one MapReduce design of TA concurrent execution in a cloud environment. The optimization of TA analysis is discussed. The proposed solutions are simulated using Hadoop in a cloud environment.

6.1 TA Concurrent Execution and Analysis

6.1.1 TA *Concurrent Execution*

Figure 6.1 shows the relationship between TA and AR. The test database that contains X, F, P, N, U tables is shared to TA and AR. TA and AR can do concurrent execution on their test workloads.[1]

As mentioned, AR needs multiple configurations to test to determine the status of interactions. Sometimes, AR needs to test thousands of configurations before it can determine the faulty interactions. In AR P is useful as it can eliminate many candidates from testing. A *Pass* in AR will result in all of sub-configurations to pass. But in TA X and F are useful as they can eliminate. One X or F can eliminate many configurations. Thus, the strategy is to wait until sufficient number of configurations (classified as U) to test, given a PTR (previous test result). Run until any interaction has been identified as X or F, and then run TA. Similarly, irrelevant configurations

---

[1]Parts of this chapter are reprinted from [1], with permission from IEEE.

© The Author(s) 2017
W. Tsai and G. Qi, *Combinatorial Testing in Cloud Computing*,
SpringerBriefs in Computer Science, https://doi.org/10.1007/978-981-10-4481-6_6

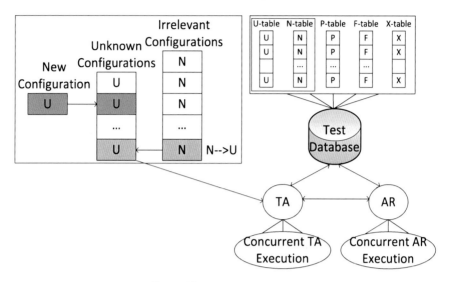

Fig. 6.1 Relationship between TA and AR

can also be eliminated from testing consideration. So only, U configurations need to be tested.

New U configurations are put into candidate configuration set. There are two types of new configurations [1]:

1. Totally new configurations (it has not been tested, even though its sub-configurations may have been tested before);
2. N configurations change to U configurations (also, some sub-configurations may have been tested before).

Figure 6.2 shows that TA and AR share the same test database that includes X, F, N, P, and U tables. When new configurations come, they are added into U configuration set as candidate testing configurations. Parts of N configurations change their statuses to NU (this is a new status and will be discussed soon) and are treated as U configurations. The NU and U configurations will be evaluated by TA and AR to identify faulty interactions using existing test results:

1. Run TA to check whether existing test results can be used to determine if the new configuration is valid. If yes, change status of new configurations from U to X or F only. It cannot be P as this is a new configuration and thus it must be tested.
2. Otherwise, wait for a sufficient number of configurations need to be tested to run AR to test new configurations. The explored test results are saved in test databases.

   - If test result of new configuration is F or X, its faulty or infeasible interaction will be identified by AR.

Fig. 6.2 Test results shared
by TA and AR

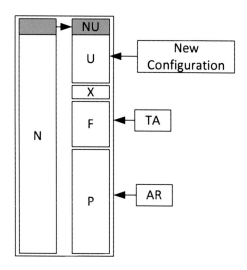

- As most configurations will be N, even if **AR** runs all the U configurations, no-faulty interactions have been identified. In this case, it is not productive to perform **TA** as **TA** needs X or F to eliminate configurations from testing. If so, we have two choices:
  - Stop testing (including both **AR** and **TA**) as no new information is available for further computation.
  - Or, convert some N configurations into U. These N configurations need not be tested, but they were tested to identify faulty interactions. They are labeled as NU (as they are actually N, but treated as U), and run **AR** with both NU and U configurations. Different algorithms can be developed to identify those N configurations to be relabeled as NU so that these NU can be tested.
3. Change interaction that changes from N or U to F or X; if **AR** is successful in identifying them, run **TA** to eliminate all related configurations from testing consideration.

6.1.2 NU Configuration

As NU configurations are added into testing consideration, the number of N configurations and the number of U configurations change.

- Number of N configurations (N′): N′ = N − NU;
- Number of U configurations (U′): U′ = U + NU.

The total number of N′ and U′ equals to the total number of N and U. The only change is the number of NU in N and U configuration sets.

6.1.3 NU *Configuration Selection Algorithms*

6.1.3.1 Random Algorithm

Random algorithm is shown in Algorithm 6 that selects configurations randomly from N configuration set and changes the selected configuration to NU. Random selection algorithm cannot involve X, F, P, and U sets.

Algorithm 6 Random Algorithm

Input:
    Irrelevant set of configurations
Output:
    Selected configurations
1: **for** int i = 0; i $\leqslant$ m; i++ **do**
2:    Randomly select one configuration out of irrelevant set
3:    Change the status of selected configuration from N to NU and return it
4: **end for**

6.1.3.2 Hamming Distance Algorithm

- **Definition**: The Hamming distance d(x, y) between two vectors $x, y \in F^{(n)}$ is the number of coefficient in which they differ where n is the number of components. For example:
  - $F^{(3)}((a, b, c), (a, b, d)) = 1$
  - $F^{(4)}((a, b, c, d), (e, f, c, d)) = 2$
- **Nearest Neighbor**: Given a code $C \in F^{(n)}$ and a vector $y \in F^{(n)}$, then $x \in C$ is a nearest neighbor to y if $d(x, y) = min(d(z, y)|z \in C)$. A vector might have more than one nearest neighbor, so a nearest neighbor is not always unique.

Find those N configurations that have minimum Hamming distance between existing F configurations, and then change their statuses to NU. The actual conditions may have different minimum Hamming distance. Using minimum Hamming distance to find those N configurations closely related to F configurations increases possibility to find those potential faulty configurations in N set.

It uses two examples to show how to use Hamming distance to select NU configurations from N configurations.

- It sets one as the default minimum Hamming distance. Select all configurations in N set that have one Hamming distance between selected faulty configuration. Change the statuses of these selected configurations from N to NU. Suppose three-way interaction (a, b, c) is faulty. (a, b, d) is one Hamming distance between interactions (a, b, c), so it can be selected as NU.

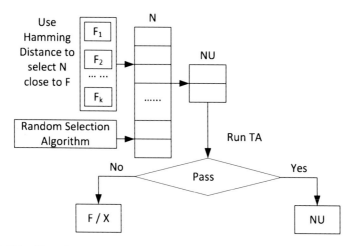

Fig. 6.3 Using Hamming distance to select NU configuration

- Figure 6.3 shows the process of finding all mutations from F interaction. Suppose two-way interaction (a_1, b_1) is faulty. Four-way interaction (a_1, b_1, c_1, d_1) is also faulty. Each component in four-way interaction has three options. One can have the following.

  - *Mutation in faulty interaction:* (a_2, b_1, c_1, d_1), (a_3, b_1, c_1, d_1), (a_1, b_2, c_1, d_1), (a_1, b_3, c_1, d_1), ... Only faulty combination part of four-way interaction mutates and the remaining part keeps same. The minimum Hamming distance is one.
  - *Mutation in both faulty and non-faulty interaction:* (a_2, b_1, c_2, d_1), (a_3, b_1, c_2, d_1), (a_1, b_2, c_1, d_2), (a_1, b_3, c_1, d_2), ... The minimum Hamming distance is two.

6.1.3.3   Mixed Strategy

The two algorithms proposed earlier can be used together. In other words, some random configurations will be used together with Hamming distance algorithm from faulty interactions with various Hamming distances, say from one to three. As often combinatorial testing has low failure rate, using the random algorithm will result in status of P often and thus speed up the AR algorithm. If the Hamming distance algorithms can detect some X or F interactions, it will help TA to eliminate configurations from testing.

Fig. 6.4 NU Configuration
selection process

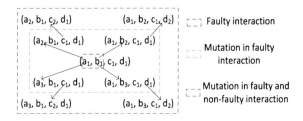

6.1.4 *Analysis Process of* NU *and* U *Configurations*

NU configuration selection process is shown in Fig. 6.4:

1. Use random algorithm or Hamming distance method to select candidate configurations from N configurations into the initial set of NU configuration.
2. Use TA to analyze the selected NU configurations.
3. If they do not pass TA analysis, they must be X or F, and they will be removed from the set of NU configurations.
4. Those that passed TA analysis can be used by AR for testing.
5. After AR testing, perform TA on those configurations that are in U or U + NU. TA can be triggered by the following two ways:

   - *On-demand*: Run TA whenever AR detects a F or X.
   - *Batch*: Run TA when AR detects a certain number of F or X, or when both U and NU have been tested completely, whatever criteria gets fulfilled. The number can be determined experimentally.

As even just one new F or X is detected by AR, numerous configurations can be removed from testing by TA, and thus even with the batch mode, the number of X or F detected need not be large.

In the integrated process, AR and TA analyses are activated by F configurations. F configurations are identified by testing. When U configurations are tested and all existing F configurations are analyzed, AR and TA analyses stop. No more related F configurations can be identified by testing analysis. For eliminating more configurations from testing considerations, it needs more F configurations to explore those N configurations.

Some N configurations that are closely related to existing F configurations can be converted into U, marked as NU, and treated as U. Test results of these NU configurations can be finalized by testing. The identified faulty NU configurations are analyzed by AR to identify the faulty root. Once the faulty root is identified, TA is activated to analyze those U configurations and eliminate related F configurations. The details of NU configurations analysis are shown in NU configurations processing algorithm.

Algorithm 7 NU Configurations Processing Algorithm

Input:
    F, N, P, U configurations
Output:
    deduced F configurations, updated U configurations
1: Run Hamming distance algorithm to find N configurations that are closely related to F configurations
2: Mark the found N configurations as NU
3: Run test cases on NU configurations
4: **if** any NU configuration is faulty **then**
5:    Run AR
6:    Return identified F interaction
7: **end if**
8: **while** all related F configurations are eliminated based on existing test results **do**
9:    **if** F interaction exists && U configuration exists **then**
10:     Run TA
11:     Return identified F configurations & updated U configurations
12:    **end if**
13: **end while**

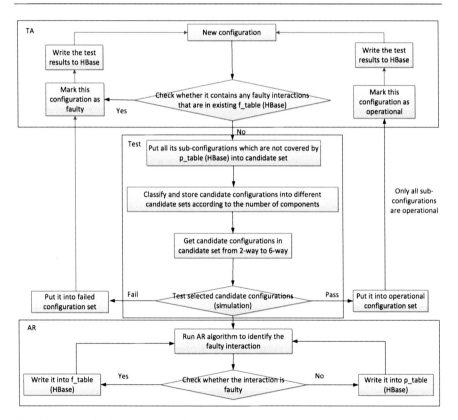

Fig. 6.5 TA MapReduce experiment flowchart

6.2   TA Experiments

6.2.1   TA *MapReduce Experiment Flowchart*

Figure 6.5 shows how the TA MapReduce experiment goes. The whole experiment executes on-demand TA analysis. Input and output of TA MapReduce experiment are as follows:

- *Input*: Configurations and seed faulty interactions;
- *Output*: TA efficiency and running time.

  Experiment environment:

- *Cluster*: 50 nodes Hadoop cluster (each node has eight processors);
- *CPU Processor*: Intel Xeon CPUE5520 2.27GHz;
- *Memory*: 11G;
- *Operating System*: CentOS release 6.3 (Final);
- *Hadoop Version*: 1.1.2;
- *HBase Version*: 0.94.12.

6.2.2   *Different Configuration Numbers of* TA *Experiments*

The first experiment is the effect of configuration number on TA efficiency. This experiment proceeds without any speedup strategy. Figure 6.6 shows that TA has a good performance on reducing test workloads. TA efficiency can also be improved a little when the number of configurations grows. The default fault rate is 0.001 in this experiment.

6.2.3   *Different Speedup Strategy for* TA *Experiments*

This experiment speeds up TA process with four different strategies (fault rate: 0.001).

- *No Strategy*: Do not use any speedup strategy;
- *Bloom Filter*: Use hash map method to store the information of interactions (bit storage);
- *Table Splitting*: Split F and P table into five tables, respectively, according to way number of interactions (from two-way to six-way);
- *Mixed Strategy*: Use Bloom Filter and Table Splitting.

Figure 6.7 compares the running time with different strategies. Bloom Filter does not affect much on running time, while Table Splitting speeds up test process significantly. Figure 6.8 shows the effect of different speedup strategies on TA efficiency. TA

Fig. 6.6 TA efficiency on Hadoop

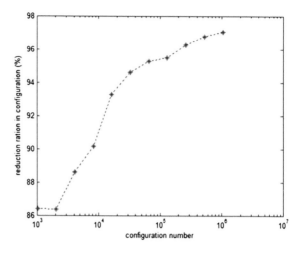

Fig. 6.7 Running time with different strategies on Hadoop

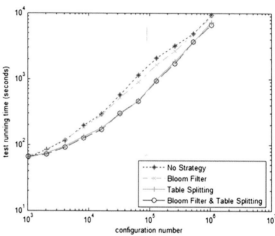

efficiency varies a little bit when configuration number is small. When configuration number increases, all strategies will have the same efficiency.

6.2.4 Different Fault Rates for TA Experiments

This experiment explores the effect of different fault rates on TA efficiency (configuration number: 524228). Figure 6.9 shows TA efficiency is affected by different fault rates. TA efficiency improves when the fault rate grows, as the fault rate can enhance F-table checking process. Figure 6.10 shows the effect of different fault rate on running time. Fault rate can decrease the running time, for the same reason.

Fig. 6.8 TA efficiency with
different strategies on
Hadoop

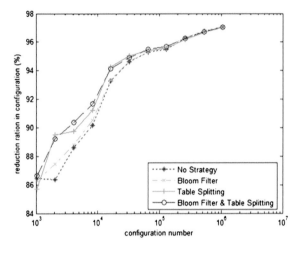

Fig. 6.9 TA efficiency with
different fault rates on
Hadoop

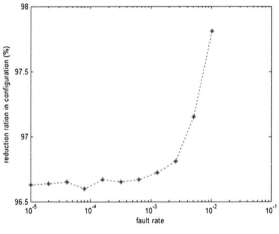

Fig. 6.10 Running time
with different fault rates on
Hadoop

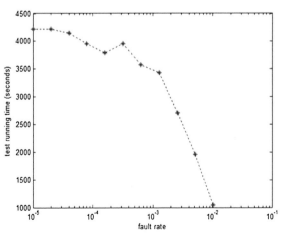

Table 6.1 Explanations of each parameter in simulation

Parameter	Meaning	Default value
$COMPONENTS\_NUMBER$	The number of components	1000
$VALUES\_NUMBER$	The values number for each component	2
$GUI\_PERCENT$	The percentage of GUI components	40%
$WORKFLOW\_PERCENT$	The percentage of workflow components	30%
$SERVICE\_PERCENT$	The percentage of service components	20%
$DATAMODEL\_PERCENT$	The percentage of data model components	10%
$TENANT\_APPLICATIONS_NUMBER$	The number of tenant applications	512
$COMPONENTS\_NUMBER\_IN\_APP$	The components number in one application	10
$ERROR\_PROBABILITY$	The fault rate	0.001

6.2.5 Explanation on Simulated Data

Table 6.1 shows the parameters used. The total number of configurations equals to the number of tenant applications powered by number of values and number of components in applications.

6.2.6 Simulation with Different Clusters

Figures 6.11 and 6.12 show the TA efficiency with different number of configurations. The x-axis represents the number of configurations, and the y-axis represents the TA efficiency. About 97% of test cases can be reduced by TA algorithm. The improvement depends upon the fault pattern and TA algorithm. Parallel implementation of TA algorithm has no contribution to the TA efficiency, although it can greatly shorten the execution time of TA processing.

6.2.7 Simulation using 37-node Cluster with Different Map Slots

The experiments were done using 37-node cluster. Figures 6.13 and 6.14 show the TA efficiency with different map slots on each machine. The x-axis represents the

Fig. 6.11 Running time of
TA implementation on
Hadoop using different
clusters

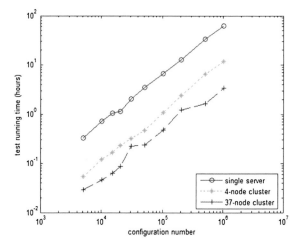
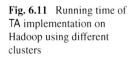

Fig. 6.12 Configuration
reduction ratio using TA
implementation on Hadoop
using different clusters

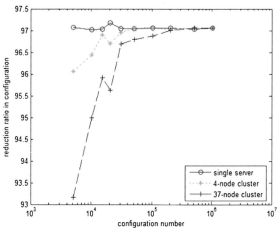

number of configurations, and the y-axis represents the TA efficiency. The number
of map slots represents the number of map tasks each machine can process at same
time. Generally, more map slots are used, the less execution time is. But, more map
slots actually contribute almost nothing to the execution time. It is probably as the
limitation of HBase ability to handle the requests. Also, more map slots have nothing
to do with the TA reduction ratio as Fig. 6.14 shows.

Fig. 6.13 Running time of
TA implementation on
Hadoop using 37-node
cluster with different map
slots

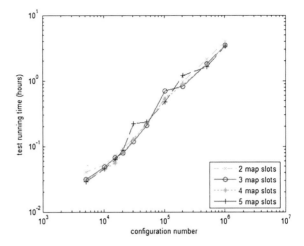

Fig. 6.14 Configuration
reduction ratio using TA
implementation on Hadoop
using 37-node cluster with
different map slots

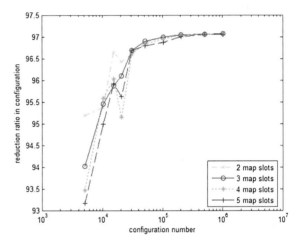

6.3   Conclusion

The TA defines five states of test results with a priority and three operations and provides a foundation for concurrent combinatorial testing. By using the TA operations,
many combinatorial tests can be eliminated as the TA identifies those interactions
that need not be tested. Also, the TA defines operation rules to merge test results
done by different processors, so that combinatorial tests can be done in a concurrent
manner. The TA rules ensure that either merged results are consistent or a testing
failure has been detected so that retest is needed. TA and AR cooperate to analyze

candidate configurations for increasing testing efficiency. In this way, large-scale combinatorial testing can be carried out in a cloud platform with a large number of processors to perform test execution in parallel to identify faulty interactions.

Reference

1. W. Wu, W.-T. Tsai, C. Jin, G. Qi, J. Luo, Test-Algebra execution in a cloud environment, in *Proceedings of 8th IEEE International Symposium on Service-Oriented System Engineering (SOSE2014)*, 2014

Chapter 7
Adaptive Reasoning Algorithm with Automated Test Cases Generation and Test Algebra in Saas System

Abstract A new integrated testing framework is proposed to use adaptive reasoning algorithm with automated test cases generation (ARP) and test algebra (TA) for increasing SaaS testing efficiency in faulty combination identification and elimination. The ARP algorithm has been evaluated by both simulation and real experimentation using a MTA SaaS sample running on GAE (Google App Engine). Both the simulation and experiment show that the ARP algorithm can identify those faulty combinations rapidly and TA can eliminate a large number of faults from candidate test set with a small number of seeded faults.

7.1 Experimentation Using a MTA SaaS Sample

This adaptive reasoning algorithm is evaluated using a sample MTA SaaS, and the SaaS was developed using the OIC framework, including customization of GUI, workflows, services, and data. The SaaS implements Arcade Game Maker (AGM) that tenant can configure their game applications and run on GAE. The games originated from software product line (SPL) system developed at the SEI/CMU.

The overall SaaS architecture is shown in Fig. 7.1. On the left side, the system handles the access control as each role has its own access right. For example, an administrator is a role to manage all the customization information of tenants, but tenants can access their own configurations only and each player can execute the game only. The system has 15 components and each component has different number of configurable values as shown in Fig. 7.2.

Assuming each component in the SaaS database has previously module tested, and thus faults in the SaaS system are those t-way component interaction faults. The number of possible configurations is 2,275,983,360. We have performed exhaustive

---

Parts of this chapter is reprinted from [1, 3], with permission from IEEE.

© The Author(s) 2017
W. Tsai and G. Qi, *Combinatorial Testing in Cloud Computing*,
SpringerBriefs in Computer Science, https://doi.org/10.1007/978-981-10-4481-6_7

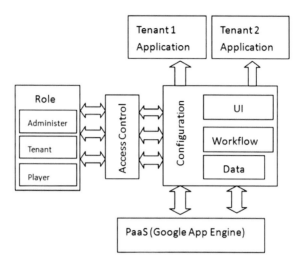

Fig. 7.1 Architecture of SUT

Object Xposition	100	200	300	400	500	600	700	
Object Yposition	100	200	300	400	500			
Object Speed	1	2	3					
Object Direction	0	30	60	90	120	180		
Object Color	Blue	Yellow	Green	Red	White	Black	Pink	Orange
Object Width	100	200						
Object Height	100	200						
Object StartMoving	TRUE	FALSE						
Screen Width	800	900	1000					
Screen Height	600	700	800					
Score of Object 1	Paddle	Puck	Ball	Bowling	Brick1	Brick2	Brick3	
Score of Object 2	Paddle	Puck	Ball	Bowling	Brick1	Brick2	Brick3	
Background Color	Blue	Yellow	Green	Red	White	Black	Pink	Orange
Control Object	Paddle	Puck	Ball	Bowling				
Game Object	Paddle	Puck	Ball	Bowling				

Fig. 7.2 All the configured components and elements

testing on these combinations to verify the SaaS system, and the faults are identified as follows:

The conflict of objects' borders: For any two objects, their starting positions may be overlapped. These kinds of faults are defined by four components, Object Xposition, Object Yposition, Object Width, and Object Height.

The conflict of objects' borders and boundary of game screen: For any objects, their starting positions might be out of game screen. These kinds of faults is defined by six components, Object Xposition, Object Yposition, Object Width, Object Height, Screen Width, and Screen Height.

The conflict of color between objects and game screen: The object color cannot be the same as background color of the game board. These kinds of faults are defined by two components, Object Color and Background Color.

The conflict of objects' width and screen width: The object width could not be wider than screen's All the configured components and elements width. These kinds of faults are defined by three components, Object Xposition, Object Width and Screen Width.

The conflict of objects' height and screen height: The object height cannot be higher than screen's height. These kinds of faults is defined by three components, Object Yposition, Object Height, and Screen Height.

The conflict of objects' Game Object and Control Object: The Game Object and Control cannot be the same one because players can control only one to win the game. These kinds of faults are defined by two components, Control Object and Game Object.

The conflict of scores of two objects: the scores of two colliding object cannot be the same and these two objects cannot be stationary. As two stationary objects cannot move so that they can never collide with each other. This kind of faults is defined by two components.

While most of faults are the results of 2-way interactions, but there are faults due to 4-way and 6-way interactions in the SaaS system. These are unknown until exhaustive testing is performed.

The AR algorithm is applied to test the SaaS system, but the experiment is limited to verify 2-way interactions to limit the computation time. The results show that using only 700 test cases, or about 0.00003% of total number of configurations, the AR algorithm detected all the 2-way interaction faults.

As we did not run t-way interaction for t ≥ 3, those faults are not identified, and thus some 3-way faults are mistaken to be 2-way faults. For example, AR verifies

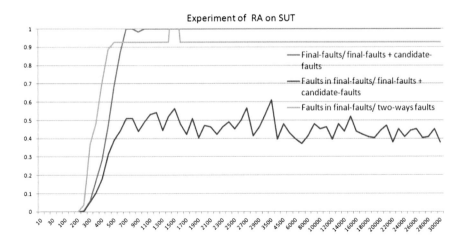

Fig. 7.3 Experiment of RA on SUT

Three configured game samples

Support function of customization

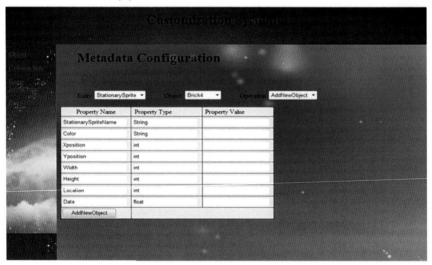

Fig. 7.4 Functions of SUT

that (A1, B2) is a fault, but it is not fault as (A1, B2, C3) is a 3-way fault. If AR performed t-ways, t ≥ 2, this situation will be eliminated.

Figure 7.3 shows that the percentage of final-faults in final-faults and candidate-faults increases with more test cases. Figure 7.4 shows the functions of SUT.

7.2   SaaS Testing

The SaaS testing flowchart is shown in Fig. 7.5. The left-hand side shows four types of tenant application components, including GUI, workflows, services, and data, and

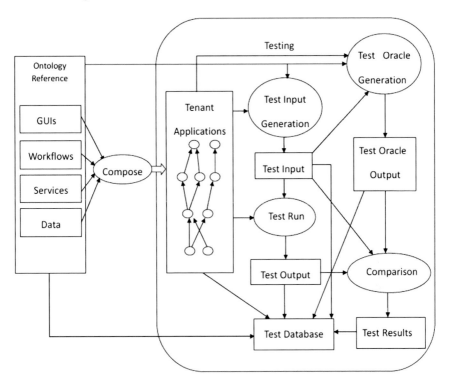

Fig. 7.5 SaaS testing flowchart

they can be used to compose tenant application according to the OIC framework [2]. The test framework consists of test input generation, expected output generation, test result evaluation, test database.

Test Input Generation: Once a tenant application is composed, test input can be generated using the ontology information to test applications. For example, GUIs, workflow, service, and data may contain constraint including data constraints and sequence constraints, and these constraints can be used to generate test inputs.

Expected Output Generation: In general, expected output generation is difficult as there is no general algorithm available today. However, in a multi-versioned environment or in regression testing, expected outputs may be obtained by voting or historical data. In a SaaS environment, the input and output of each component can be tracked and recorded during program execution, and thus after execution of tenant applications multiple times, the input and output of each constituent component can be recorded for regression testing. This approach is also taken by IKTO in a service-oriented environment.

Test Result Evaluation: After test run, the test output is compared with the expected output.

Test Database: The database contains tenant application configuration, test inputs, outputs, expected outputs, and results. The database design for tenant application configuration is most important consideration, and it needs to address the following three issues:

- **Configuration Storage for t-way interactions (Configuration Table)**: For each tenant, it is necessary to evaluate all t-way interaction for $t \geqslant 2$, faults among components within the tenant configuration. One way to store configuration is to use hypergraph, a hypergraph is a graph model where a link can have more than two nodes. Specifically, 2-node link can represent a 2-way interaction, a 3-node link a 3-way interaction, and so on.
- **Previous failed t-way interactions (F-Table)**: According to TA for a tenant application to pass the testing, it needs to pass all t-way interaction testing, starting from 2-way all the way to k-way interactions where k is the number of components in the tenant application. Thus, if a t-way interaction fault is detected, the testing can bet stopped as the tenant application already failed the test. The F table contains a list of failed t-way interactions, and each is a minimal fault. For example, if 3-way interaction (a, b, c) is in the F-table, it means there are no 2-way faults among a, b, and c. The key is to identify those failed t-way interactions rapidly.
- **Previous passed t-way interactions (P-Table)**: According to three principles, if a t-way interaction has passed the testing, this information will be useful to reduce testing effort according to the AR algorithm. The idea is to identify those t-way interactions efficiently.

Optimization: One can improve Configuration Table, F-Table, and P-Table by arranging them in the order of usage frequency. We set different weight value between nodes to stand for frequency of use in this combination. If the weight value is lower, it means this combination is used more frequent. So it should first take these combinations into consideration when conducting testing. As for these low weight combinations, it is so urgent to detect whether they are faults or not because few tenants use them. In this testing framework, a recommendation model would be imported according the weight value of combinations. If the weight value is high, it means more tenants would like to use them, so system should recommend to other tenants when they conduct configuration. For these low weight combinations, their prior of recommendation and test is lower.

7.3 SaaS Test Case Generation

If a configuration passed the testing, all of its t-way interactions are not faulty, and thus all of them will be placed in a set of non-fault. If a configuration fails the testing, all of its t-way interactions will be a candidate-faulty, and thus all these t-way interactions are placed in a set of candidate-fault. Only the failed configuration with only one interaction can be stored in the final-fault set. A fault is a bug in the system, and a final-fault is a fault that has been detected by the AR algorithm. Thus, $|final - faultset| \leq |faultset|$. As AR executes, the number of final-faults will increase until all the faults are identified. As AR executes, the set of candidate-fault initially increases, and as each candidate-fault will be eliminated by further testing, the set will eventually decrease. At the end, the candidate-fault set will be empty. AR algorithm not only finds the faulty configurations, but also gets which part of the configuration causes the fault. For example, there are four functional units (a, b, c, d) and each unit has five options. So there are 54 configurations in total. If in 2-way testing the configuration (a_1, b_1, c_1, d_1) is wrong and only the combination of (a_1, b_1) is wrong, (a_1, b_1, c_1, d_1) can be stored in the final-fault set. It should not only prove (a_1, b_1) is wrong, but also prove the other 2-way combinations are correct including $(a_1, c_1), (a_1, d_1), (b_1, c_1), (b_1, d_1)$, and (c_1, d_1). The similarly testing should be taken in 3-way, 4-way, and even k-way testing to cover all possible configurations to make sure that all faulty combinations are eliminated. The automated test case generation algorithm generates the test cases first. Then system uses AR algorithm to do testing with the generated test cases. During the testing process, system updates the stored information to make sure that pairs of $P_{i,j}$ in final-fault would not appear in T_m. The parameters in Algorithm 1:

Algorithm 8 Automated Test Case Generation Algorithm

1: get one element $(P_{m,n}, P_{x,y})$ candidate-fault random
2: **for** each P_i (except P_m and P_x) in test case **do**
3:   repeat
4:     initialize SE (Stack Element) to store each possible value for P_i
5:     **for** j=0; j$< P_i(max)$; j++ **do**
6:       repeat
7:         **if** $(P_{i,j}, P_{m,n})$ and $(P_{i,j}, P_{x,y})$ and $(P_{i,j}, P_{k,j})$ $(0 < k < i)$ exist in no-fault **then**
8:           set the value of P_i to $P_{i,j}$
9:           break and set the value of next component
10:        **else if** $(P_{i,j}, P_{m,n})$ and $(P_{i,j}, P_{x,y})$ and $(P_{i,j}, P_{k,j})$ $(0 < k < i)$ do not exist in candidate-fault **then**
11:          add the $P_{i,j}$ in SE
12:        **end if**
13:    **end for**
14:    **if** P_i is null **then**
15:      set the value of P_i to one of element in SE randomly
16:    **else if** SE is null **then**
17:      generate the value of P_i randomly
18:    **end if**
19: **end for**

- $P = P_i$ is set of parameters as configurable components, where $0 < i \leqslant n$ and n is the number of components.
- $P_i = P_{i,j}$ is set of values for component P_i, where $0 < j \leqslant P_i(Max)$. $P_i(Max)$ is the number of value in component P_i.

- $T = T_m$ is a test case which contains $P_{1,j}, P_{2,j},..., P_{n,j}$, where $0 < m \leqslant TN$ and $0 < j \leqslant P_i(Max)$. TN is the number of test case.

After finishing testing, the elements will be updated in the final-fault list.

In automated test case generation algorithm, the test generation only ensures that each composition of $P_{i,j}$ and $P_{m,n}$, $P_{i,j}$ and $P_{x,y}$ exist in no-fault. Since it is not easy to ensure that each composition exists in no-fault except $(P_{m,n}, P_{i,j})$, it only talks about the interaction of $P_{m,n}$ and $P_{i,j}$ with other $P_{i,j}$. This method is easy to do and saves a lot of time in calculation.

$P = P_i$ is set of parameters as configurable components, where $0 < i \leqslant n$ and n is the number of component.

$P_i = P_{i,j}$ is set of values for component Pi, where $0 < j \leqslant P_i(Max)$. $P_i(Max)$ is the number of value in component P_i.

$T = T_m$ is a test case which contains $P_{1,j}, P_{2,j},..., P_{n,j}$, where $0 < m \leqslant TN$ and $0 < j \leqslant P_i(Max)$.

TN is the number of test case.

Final-fault is the list of compositions of $(P_{i,j}, P_{x,y})$ which are generated by RA and verified by RA that they would cause the failure of system, where $0 < j \leqslant P_i(Max)$, $0 < y \leqslant P_x(Max), 0 < i \leqslant n, 0 < x \leqslant n, x \neq i$.

Candidate-fault is the list of compositions of $(P_{i,j}, P_{x,y})$ which are generated by RA. It is highly possible that they would cause the failure of system, but RA is not sure about it, where $0 < j \leqslant P_i(Max), 0 < y \leqslant P_x(Max), 0 < i \leqslant n, 0 < x \leqslant n, x \neq i$.

No-fault is the list of compositions of $(P_{i,j}, P_{x,y})$ which are verified that they would not cause the failure of system, where $0 < j \leqslant P_i(Max), 0 < y \leqslant P_x(Max), 0 < i \leqslant n, 0 < x \leqslant n, x \neq i$.

C_n is the number of elements in candidate-fault. C_m represents that when C_n is equal or larger than C_m, the algorithm would begin the auto-random process of test case generation.

Test case generation is different with that in AR. AR algorithm uses a random method to generate test cases while AR algorithm with automated test cases generation (marked as ARP) achieves a different strategy. The way is that ARP selects one composition in candidate-faults while other combinations come from no-faults. System could detect whether this candidate-fault is final-fault or not. If the test case failed, it is final-fault because other combinations are no-faults. Otherwise it is no-fault.

However, test generation cannot ensure that all the generated test cases meet the scenario above. It is easy to select one composition from candidate-faults while it is not easy to ensure that all other combinations could be chosen from no-faults and all the chosen combinations in candidate-faults and no-faults could make up a test case. For example, there are five components: a, b, c, d, e, and each component has three values of configuration. If there are no combinations both in candidate-faults and no-faults, which composed of any values (e_1, e_2, e_3) in e, it is impossible to generate such a test case by following the above-mentioned method.

Algorithm 9 ARP Algorithm

Require:
    the set of configurable components P_i and each $P_{i,j}$ for P_i, where $0 < i \leqslant n, 0 < j \leqslant P_i(max)$
Ensure:

- final-fault (a list of composition of two components which are verified by RA as faults)
- candidate-fault (a list of composition of two components which are possible as faults in system)
- no-fault (a list of composition of two components which are not faults)

1: **while** m < TN **do**
2:   **if** $C_m < C_n$ **then**
3:     generate the value randomly for each $P_{i,j}$ as an new test case T_m
4:   **else**
5:     generate test case T
6:   **end if**
7:   **if** final-fault contains the composition of $P_{i,j}$ in T_m **then**
8:     break and generate another test case
9:   **end if**
10:   **if** T_m causes the failure in system **then**
11:     **for** each composition of $P_{i,j}$ in T_m **do**
12:       repeat
13:       **if** composition of ($P_{i,j}$, $P_{x,y}$) is not in candidate-fault and composition ($P_{i,j}$, $P_{x,y}$) is not in final-fault and composition of ($P_{i,j}$, $P_{x,y}$) is not in no-fault **then**
14:         add ($P_{i,j}$, $P_{x,y}$) in candidate-fault
15:       **end if**
16:     **end for**
17:   **else**
18:     **for** each composition of $P_{i,j}$ in T_m **do**
19:       repeat
20:       **if** composition of ($P_{i,j}$, $P_{x,y}$) is in candidate-fault **then**
21:         remove ($P_{i,j}$, $P_{x,y}$) in candidate-fault
22:         add ($P_{i,j}$, $P_{x,y}$) in no-fault
23:       **end if**
24:     **end for**
25:   **end if**
26:   **for** r=0; $r < m$; r++ **do**
27:     repeat
28:     **if** T_r causes the failure in system **then**
29:       **for** each composition of $P_{i,j}$ in T_r **do**
30:         **if** there is only one ($P_{i,j}$, $P_{x,y}$) in candidate-fault **then**
31:           remove ($P_{i,j}$, $P_{x,y}$) in candidate-fault
32:           add ($P_{i,j}$, $P_{x,y}$) in final-fault
33:         **end if**
34:       **end for**
35:     **end if**
36:   **end for**
37:   m++
38: **end while**

To solve the problem above, we design an algorithm that most of combinations come from no-faults and the rest of combinations are not from candidate-faults. The design of algorithm is shown in Algorithm 2. First of all, a composition is chosen from candidate-fault randomly. Then, other values in one element are chosen by obeying the following rules:

1. If the combinations of this value and other values in the chosen candidate-fault exist in no-faults, set the value to this element.
2. If the above scenario does not meet, check whether these combinations exist in candidate-faults. If they are in the candidate-faults, add this value in a candidate queue SE. Otherwise check the next value.
3. If the value has not be chosen, set the value to one element in SE randomly.
4. If the SE is empty, set the value randomly.

The **ARP** algorithm is shown in Algorithms 8 and 9. In the test generation, we achieve half automatic and half random test case generation. Because there must be some candidate-faults and no-faults when using automatic test generation. However, no candidate-faults and no-faults exist at the initiation. So random test case generation is needed and we combine these two methods in test generation. T_s is the number of a group of test cases. In one group, half of test cases are generated by automatic test case generation and others are generated randomly. Test generation are conducted by groups one by one. The value of T_s can be defined by users.

7.4   Simulation and Analysis

7.4.1   Simulation of ARP Algorithm

The **ARP** algorithm is simulated on a system with 15 components and every component has 10 values that could be chosen by tenants. The number of possible composition is 1,000 trillion and all possible two-way faults are 10,500. **ARP** is used to detect all the possible faults in test cases and would stop when all faults are found. The value of T_S is two hundred.

To test the faulty analysis ability of **ARP** and **TA** it only sets initial faults in candidate test set. Table 7.1 shows the number of 2-way to 6-way interactions. Table 7.2 shows the number of seeded faults and the corresponding distributions. It increases the number of faults from 100 to 300. The corresponding percentages of seeded faults over all 2-way to 6-way interactions are $1.88*10^{-6}\%$, $3.76*10^{-6}\%$, and $5.64*10^{-6}\%$, respectively.

In the simulation, we compare **ARP** with **AR** to show the enhancement in performance. We simulate **ARP** and **AR** when there are different faults in configuration. The number of faults are 100, 200, 300, respectively. We find **ARP** is more efficient with more faults.

Table 7.1 The number of T-way interactions from 2-way to 6-way in SaaS example

Range	Size
2-way interactions	10,500
3-way interactions	455,000
4-way interactions	13,650,000
5-way interactions	300,300,000
6-way interactions	5,005,000,000
Interactions from 2-way to 6-way	5,319,415,500

Table 7.2 The initial setting ups of faulty interactions in SaaS example

Range	100 Faults	200 Faults	300 Faults	Distribution percentage (%)
2-way interactions	50	100	150	50
3-way interactions	27	54	81	27
4-way interactions	20	40	60	20
5-way interactions	2	4	6	2
6-way interactions	1	2	3	1

Figure 7.6 shows the result of final-faults/faults in ARP and AR. Y-axis is final-faults/faults. X-axis is the number of test cases. When faults are only 100, the performance of AR is almost the same with ARP, even AR is better than ARP in some points. However, when the number of faults increases, ARP finds more faults than AR with the same number of test case. For example, AR find only 0.5% faults while ARP has already found 37.5% faults. The performance of ARP is even better with more faults. For example, when the number of faults reaches 300, ARP finds 98% faults with 6000 test cases while AR only find 0.3% faults.

Figure 7.7 shows the comparison of final-faults/(final-faults+candidate-faults) between ARP and AR. X-axis is the number of test case, and Y-axis is final-faults/(final-faults+candidate-faults). The result of comparison is almost the same with that in Fig. 7.6. The performance of ARP is better than AR.

Figure 7.8 shows the test configuration failure percentage. X-axis is the number of test case and y-axis is failed test cases/all test cases. The failure percentage in ARP is lower than that in AR with 100, 200, 300 faults, respectively. It indicates that when more no-failure test cases are generated, it is easier to detect more faults. Because there are more no-failure test cases, more combinations are added into no-faults. So it is easier to detect whether candidate-faults are final-faults or not with more no-faults.

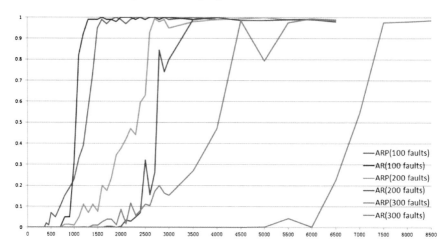

Fig. 7.6 Final-Faults/Faults

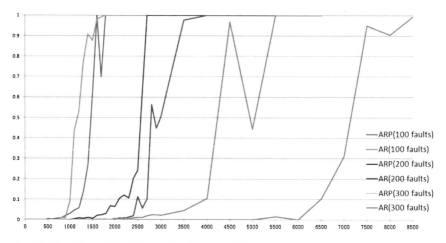

Fig. 7.7 Final-Faults/(Final-Faults+Candidate-Faults)

7.4.2 *Incremental Testing with Automatic Test Generation*

A SaaS system allows tenant developers to upload their components into the SaaS database, and these new components can interact with the existing components causing new tenant applications to fail. The AR algorithm can be run in an incremental manner to handle new components whenever new components are added.

When SaaS systems start to operate with few initial tenant components, the ARP algorithm can be run and the testing results are kept in the database. When new components are added, the ARP algorithm can be run, instead of starting from

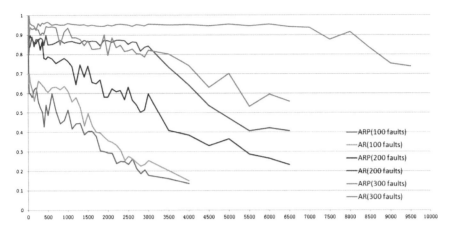

Fig. 7.8 Test configuration failure percentage

the scratch, using the stored test results (no-faults and final-faults) to speed up the processing. This approach is labeled as $ARP + PTR$ (previous test results).

The $ARP + PTR$ algorithm also uses the automatic test case generation in test generation. It is different with $AR + PTR$ that use a random way in test generation. $ARP + PTR$ aims at lower failure percentage so that it is easier for system to detect more final-faults with the same test cases.

7.4.3 Simulation Experiments of ARP+PTR

The configuration in $ARP + PTR$ is 15 components and each component has 10 values. In the 15 components, 5 components are added into the system as new components while another 10 components have already existed in the previous configuration. All the faults in these 10 components have been detected and would not occur in the test generation.

To compare the performance between $ARP + PTR$ and $AR + PTR$, we set different numbers of faults in the simulation: 150, 200, 300, and 400. The value of T_s is two hundred.

Figure 7.9 shows the result of final-faults/faults. When there are 150 faults, the performance of $ARP + PTR$ and $AR + PTR$ are almost same. However, $ARP + PTR$ outperforms $AR + PTR$ with 200, 300, 400 faults in configuration. For example, when there are 200 faults, $ARP + PTR$ finds 86% faults with 2,100 test cases while $AR + PTR$ find 25% faults. With more faults in configuration, the performance of $ARP + PTR$ is better. When there are 400 faults, $ARP + PTR$ finds 96.5% faults while $AR + PTR$ finds 0% faults.

Figure 7.10 shows the result of final-faults/(candidate-faults+final-faults). The trend of curve is almost the same with Fig. 7.9.

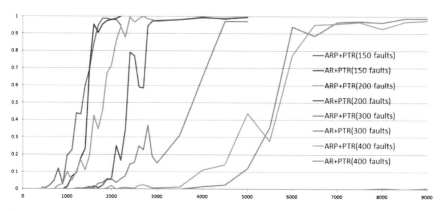

Fig. 7.9 Final-faults/faults

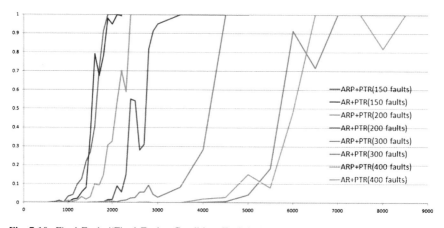

Fig. 7.10 Final-Faults/(Final-Faults+Candidate-Faults)

When it comes to Fig. 7.11, it shows test configuration failure percentage. It proves the same conclusion what we prove in Fig. 7.8. If more generated test cases are not failure, more final-faults are detected.

7.4.4 Analysis of the Strategy on Test Generation

In the simulation of ARP and $ARP + PTR$, we use a strategy of combining half automatic and half random ways in test case generation. Although they outperform AR and $AR + PTR$, perhaps there are better design and strategy on the test generation.

From the data shown in Figs. 7.6 and 7.9, we find the performance of ARP and $ARP + PTR$ is more better than AR and $AR + PTR$ when there are more faults.

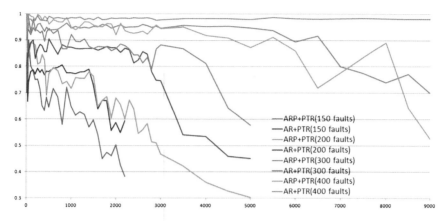

Fig. 7.11 Test configuration failure percentage

The main reason for this is that ARP and $ARP + PTR$ decrease the failure percentage that shows in Figs. 7.8 and 7.11. With more no-failure test cases, the number of no-faults increases quickly and more final-faults would be found. When there are more faults in configuration, the failure percentage of AR and $AR + PTR$ in test cases are very high. However, with automatic test case generation, ARP and $ARP + PTR$ could reduce the failure percentage significantly. When there are less faults, the failure percentage of test cases are almost same in ARP and AR. It results in that the performance of ARP and AR are almost same as data shown in Figs. 7.6 and 7.9.

To find a better strategy in test case generation, we would discuss the percentage of automatic and random ways we achieve in test generation. AR achieves only random ways in test generation while ARP combines automatic and random ways in test generation. If the percentage of automatic ways in test generation is higher, would performance of ARP be better? What effect the percentage of automatic ways has on the performance of algorithm?

This paper conducts the experiment based on the hypothesis above. We only simulate ARP in this experiment. In the configuration, there are 15 components and each component has 10 values. So the total possible combinations are 1,000 trillion and the number of faults in the experiment is 100 and 300, respectively.

The result of experiment is shown in Figs. 7.12 and 7.13. The x-axis is the number of test cases and the y-axis is final-faults/faults. 75% automatic test generation means that there are 75% test cases generated by automatic ways and the rest of test cases are generated randomly.

From Fig. 7.12, if the percentage of automatic test generation is lower, the performance of ARP is better and more final-faults are found with the same number of test cases. The situation is totally different with that in Fig. 7.13. The result in Fig. 7.13 shows that when it uses the method of automatic test generation more, the performance of ARP is better.

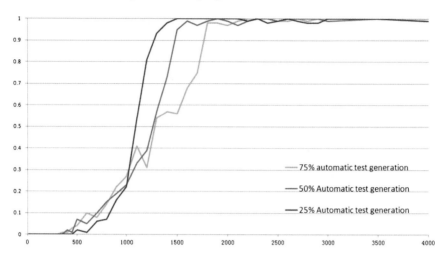

Fig. 7.12 ARP Algorithm with 100 faults

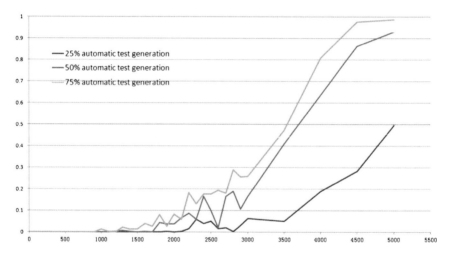

Fig. 7.13 ARP Algorithm with 300 faults

The reason for this result is that automatic test generation is more helpful to find more final-faults when there are more faults in configuration. However, when there are less faults in system, random test generation is more efficient. Because most of combinations in test cases comes from no-faults and candidate-faults when using automatic test generation. These combinations have already appeared in previous test cases and the rest of faults might exist in other combinations. Random method would generate more combinations which are not in no-faults and candidate-faults. So it could detect more final-faults with these new combinations.

Table 7.3   The reduced interactions with different fault settings

	100 Faults	200 Faults	300 Faults
Reduced interactions	$6.99*10^8$	$1.40*10^9$	$2.10*10^9$
Reduced workloads percentage (%)	13.14	26.27	39.41

7.4.5   TA *Simulation in SaaS*

Based on the initial fault settings, the number of reduced interactions and deduction rate are shown in Table 7.3. Although the initial fault rate is extremely low, TA still has good fault deduction performance. 13.14%, 26.27%, and 39.41% of candidate interactions are eliminated, respectively, by TA analysis. The fault deduction rate improves when the number of initial faults increases.

References

1. W.-T. Tsai, G. Qi, Integrated adaptive reasoning testing framework with automated fault detection, in *Proceedings of IEEE Symposium on Service-Oriented System Engineering (SOSE2015)*, pp. 169–178. IEEE, 2015
2. W.-T. Tsai, Q. Shao, W. Li, OIC: Ontology-based intelligent customization framework for SaaS, in *Proceedings of International Conference on Service Oriented Computing and Applications(SOCA'10)*, Perth, Australia, 2010
3. W.-T. Tsai, Q. Li, C.J. Colbourn, X. Bai, Adaptive fault detection for testing tenant applications in multi-tenancy SaaS systems, in *Proceedings of IEEE International Conference on Cloud Engineering (IC2E)*, 2013

Chapter 8
TaaS Design for Combinatorial Testing

Abstract Testing-as-a-Service (TaaS) in a cloud environment can leverage the computation power provided by the cloud. Specifically, testing can be scaled to large and dynamic workloads, executed in a distributed environment with hundreds of thousands of processors, and these processors may support concurrent and distributed test execution and analysis. TaaS may be implemented as SaaS and used to test SaaS applications. This chapter proposes a TaaS design for SaaS combinatorial testing. TA and AR algorithm are used in the TaaS design.

8.1 TaaS Introduction

Several TaaS definitions are available [1, 2]. It often means that testing will be online, composable, Web-based, on demand, scalable, running in a virtualized and secure cloud environment with virtually unlimited computing, storage and networking. This paper proposes a TaaS definition from two perspectives: **user's point of view** and cloud **internal point of view**.

From **user's point of view**, TaaS provides the following four services.

Test Case and Script Development: Users can develop, debug, and evaluate test cases/script online using automated tools in a collaborative manner. Test scripts may even be developed by customizing/composing existing components following the MTA approach.

Test Script Compilation and Deployment: Test scripts can be compiled and deployed for execution in a cloud environment, and TaaS resource management can allocate and reclaim resources to meet the changing workload.

Test Script Execution: Test can be executed in parallel or in a distributed manner, and it can be triggered autonomously or on demand.

Parts of this chapter is reprinted from [4], with permission from IEEE

© The Author(s) 2017   101
W. Tsai and G. Qi, *Combinatorial Testing in Cloud Computing*,
SpringerBriefs in Computer Science, https://doi.org/10.1007/978-981-10-4481-6_8

Test Result Evaluation: Cloud-based test database is built to support automated data saving, intelligent retrieval, concurrent transaction, parallel processing, and timely analysis of huge test results.

From cloud **internal point of view**, TaaS may have the following features common to most cloud operations.

Decentralized Operations: Testing tasks may be executed in a parallel or a distributed manner, migrated to dynamic allocated resources, and performed in a redundant manner, or embedded within other cloud operations.

Metadata-based Computing: Controller uses metadata to control test operations such as time, frequency, multi-tasking, redundancy, parallel execution. TaaS metadata may include information about test scripts, cases, environment, and results such as index, location, and organization.

Data-centric Testing: Big Test handles large sets of input data and produces large sets of test results. Techniques for Big Data storage, processing, and understanding are key to TaaS. For examples, test data can be saved in in-memory databases, classified by attributes (such as hot, warm, or cold), and analyzed in real-time.

Multi-tenancy Test Script Composition: Like tenant applications in a MTA SaaS platform, test scripts in a TaaS system may share the same test script base.

Automated Test Redundancy Management and Recovery: Testing tasks can be partitioned and sent to different processors for parallel and redundant processing. Test and test results can be recovered in case of failures in a processor or in a cluster due to automated redundancy management. Recovery can follow the metadata-based approach.

Automated Test Scalability: When the SUT (System Under Test) scales up at runtime in a cloud environment, TaaS also needs to scale up proportionally using common cloud scalability mechanisms such as 2-level scalability architecture and stateless service design [3].

8.2   TaaS Design with TA and AR

This section presents a new TaaS design for combinatorial testing using TA and AR. Figure 8.1 shows a TaaS design with six parts [4]. There are SaaS components DB, Test Processing, AR, TA, Test Database, and Recommendation system.

Part I SaaS Components DB: Each tenant application in SaaS has components from four layers: GUIs, workflows, services, and data.

Part II Test Processing: It uses the following components to process SaaS combinatorial testing.

Test Workloads Dispatcher: All testing workloads are sent to test dispatchers. Test dispatchers assign workloads to Test Engines according to the computation capacity

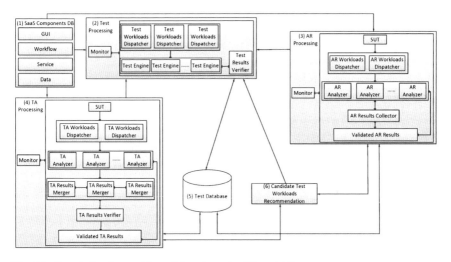

Fig. 8.1 Taas design for combinatorial testing using TA and AR

of each Test Engine. The same workloads may be executed on different Test Engines for redundant testing.

- Input: candidate configurations, the number of Test Engines, the computation capacity of each engine; and
- Output: the amount of candidate configurations assigned to each Test Engine.

Test Engine: It runs different test cases to test the assigned workloads. Test results are sent to Test Results Verifier.

- Input: the assigned candidate configurations, test cases; and
- Output: test results of the assigned candidate configurations.

Test Results Verifier: It verifies all returned test results. For the same configuration, it may have different returned test results from different Test Engines. Test Result Verifiers finalizes the correct test result based on the confidence of each test result. Only those highly confident test results are saved in the Test Database and can be shared with others. If test results verifier cannot verify the returned test results, it requires Test Engines to retest these configurations.

- Input: test results from different Test Engines; and
- Output: finalized test results.

Monitor: It monitors the testing process. Test Workloads Dispatcher, Testing Work-loads, and their related Test Engines are monitored. Each Test Engine is monitored during the testing process. Test Results Verifier is also monitored.

Part III AR Processing: It is used to figure out faulty configurations from the candidate set rapidly based on the existing test results.

SUT: It is the candidate test set.

AR *Workloads Dispatcher*: It works similarly as the Test Workloads Dispatcher of Test Processing. Different amount of candidate testing workloads are assigned to different **AR** Analyzers based on the computation capacity.

AR *Analyzer*: It runs **AR** algorithm on candidate configurations based on the existing test results. The analyzed test results are sent to the collector. It also reanalyzes those returned incorrect test results that did not pass validation.

- Input: existing test results, candidate configurations; and
- Output: test results of assigned candidate configurations.

AR *Results Collector*: It collects all test results from different **AR** Analyzers. Collector also sends those candidate configurations that cannot pass test results validation to their related **AR** analyzers.

Validated **AR** *Results*: They save all validated **AR** results and send them to the shared test database. The saved validated results are shared to all **AR** analyzers.

Monitor: It is similar as monitor of Test Processing. The process of **AR** Analysis is monitored.

Part IV TA Processing: It analyzes test results by TA. Similar to AR Processing, TA also has SUT, test dispatcher, and monitor. Their functions are same as the corresponding parts in AR. The other parts of TA have their own features.

TA *Analyzer*: It runs **TA** to analyze the test results of candidate test set based on the existing test results. Test results of those candidate configurations related to existing X or F interactions can be finalized.

- Input: existing test results, candidate configurations; and
- Output: test results of candidate configurations, candidate interactions.

TA *Results Merger*: It merges the returned from different **TA** analyzers by three defined operations. The merged test results are sent to test result verifier.

- Input: test results from different analyzers; and
- Output: merged test results.

TA *Results Verifier*: It verifies all returned test results. Usually test results with high confidence are treated as correct test results. Those test results that cannot be verified are sent back to **TA** analyzer for re-analyzing.

- Input: merged test results; and
- Output: verified test results, unverified test results.

Validated **TA** *Results*: They save and share all validated test results. The validated test results are categorized according the number of components.

Part V Test Database: It not only saves test results from Testing Processing, but also saves analyzed test results from AR and TA. Only validated test results can be saved in Test Database. All saved test results are shared and can be reused. Different from traditional databases, the saved test results are categorized by type and the number of components. For instance, 2-way and 3-way F configurations are saved in its own table respectively. Due to the large number of test results, only the roots of X, and F configurations are saved in test database. For example, configuration (a, b, c, d, e) is F and configuration (a, b, c) is the faulty root, so only configuration (a, b, c) is saved in F data table. Test results of those configurations that contain configuration (a, b, c) are automatically considered as fault.

Part VI Candidate Test Workloads Recommendation: It is used to figure out those priority configurations for testing. Based on the existing test results, it recommends those potential faults in the candidate set. Those configurations in candidate set that have one or two Hamming Distance between existing faulty configurations are recommended for TA and AR. TA, AR and Recommendation system communicate often. TA and AR send their analyzed test results to Recommendation system. Recommendation system sends related candidate configurations to them. Comparing TA and AR, the communication between Test Engine and Recommendation system is one-way direction. Only Recommendation system sends candidate configurations to Test Engine. The parent sets of faulty configurations found by AR are recommended to Test Engine for testing.

Confidence: Confidence is used to measure the reliability of each configuration's test result. Confidence (C) is the ratio of the number of one type test result (T) in all returned test results (AT) of one configuration. $C(T_i) = \frac{T_i}{AT} = \frac{T_i}{\sum_{i=1}^{n} T_i}$, and $\sum_{i=1}^{n} C(T_i) = 1$, i is number of different types T. The confidence $C(T_i)$ measures are bounded by the interval [0,1].

For example, one test workload is processed on three virtual machines a, b, and c respectively. Machine a, b, and c return m, n, and m as results respectively. Three tests have two test results m and n. Two machines return m, about 66.6% of all test results. Test result m that has higher confidence than result n is treated as the verified test result. If test results cannot be finalized, those combinations must be tested again, until the their test result can be finalized.

8.3   TaaS as SaaS

A TaaS can be implemented as a SaaS. Table 8.1 shows the comparison between SaaS and TaaS. Similar to other SaaS systems, a TaaS database also has four layers: GUIs, workflows, services, and data. It also has three important characteristics, customization, multi-tenancy, and scalability. TaaS allows tenants to compose their TaaS applications using the existing testing services.

Table 8.1 SaaS and TaaS comparison

	SaaS	TaaS
Automated provisioning	SaaS automatically adjusts the computing resources following the change of workloads. It scales up with increasing loads with automated expansion. Vice verse, it scales down	TaaS supports automated provisioning and de-provisioning of computing resources in a scalable cloud test environment
Migration	Each unit of data can be moved for scalability	The migration process can be monitored, traced, and tested
Automated load balancing	It automatically balances the workloads across multiple virtual machines	Balanced testing workloads are assigned to different servers
Composition	The complicated services are composed by basic functional services.	Based on the candidate test workloads, the specific TaaS is also composed by basic testing services
Concurrent	The workloads of SaaS can be executed concurrently on different servers	Testing workloads can be distributed to different servers and processed at the same time
Crash and recovery	When crash happens, SaaS can be recovered from backup copies on different servers	TaaS uses backup copies to recover from crash automatically

Figure 8.2 shows a TaaS infrastructure. It has two parts, one is the runtime platform, the other one is the customization & runtime repositories. The *Runtime platform* performs six functions.

- Scheduling: The order of TA analysis, AR analysis, and testing are scheduled according to the existing test results. New verified test results are updated and shared in a time manner.
- Provisioning: The computation resources are provided to the designated test workloads on demand.
- Monitoring: All TaaS-related activities are monitored.
- Load Balancing: Test workloads are assigned to each server according its computation capacity.
- Verification: All test results need to be validated, and only validated test results are saved.
- Recommendation: The recommendation mechanism uses algorithms to analyze candidate configurations. Then it recommends those selected candidate configurations for retesting.

The *Customization & runtime repositories* have TaaS four-layer model as traditional SaaS. Each layer provides different options for tenants to compose their own TaaS applications. The ontology & Linked Data guides the TaaS composition process.

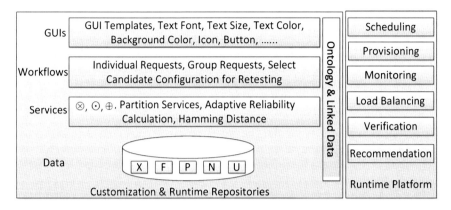

Fig. 8.2 TaaS infrastructure

8.3.1 GUIs

Various TaaS templates are stored in the GUI repository, tenants can build their own GUIs based on the templates. Tenants can customize the existing templates, such as modifying text font and size. Commonly use operations of changing and configuring GUI appearance, such as adding/editing/deleting icons, colors, fonts, titles in pages, menus and page-section are available.

8.3.2 Workflows

Individual request: It involves testing single configurations. TA analyzes single configurations first. If its test result can be determined from existing test results, there is no need to do any testing. Otherwise, the configuration needs to be tested.

Group request: This involves testing of multiple configurations. The following procedures shows the steps.

1. Partition the space: Due to heavy workloads, the workloads are partitioned and assigned to different Test Engines for processing. One configuration may be assigned to multiple Test Engines for redundant testing. The partitioning process intelligently adjusts the workloads according to the computation capacity of each Test Engine.
2. Evaluation operations $\otimes$ and $\odot$: The assigned workloads should be analyzed by TA first. The test results are saved in the Test Database.
3. Merge operation $\oplus$: $\oplus$ operation is used to merge testing results from different Test Engines.

4. Store consistent results: When it merges testing results from different Test Engines. Reliability of these results is computed, and only highly confident results are stored in the database (Fig. 8.3).
5. Send for retesting: Those configurations with uncertain test results will be sent back for further testing.

Select Candidate Configurations for Retesting: While a large number of configurations needs to be tested, but the number of faulty configurations is only a small percentage of configurations. It is difficult to find these faulty configurations. NU configurations are added into testing consideration for increasing the chance of finding faulty configurations. NU configurations are from N configurations, but are treated as U configurations. Based on the existing F configurations, different algorithms such as Random, Hamming Distance, and mixed strategies can be used to get NU configurations from N configurations [5].

8.3.3 Services

$\otimes$ *Operation Service*: It is used to get the test result of $V(\mathscr{T}_1 \cup \mathscr{T}_2)$ from $V(\mathscr{T}_1)$ and $V(\mathscr{T}_2)$.

$\odot$ *Operation Service*: Test result of one configuration can be composed by merging tests results of all its interactions, such as $V(\mathscr{T}) = \odot_{\mathscr{I} \subseteq \mathscr{T}} V(\mathscr{I})$, where $\mathscr{I}$ is an interaction covered by configuration $\mathscr{T}$.

$\oplus$ *Operation Service*: It merges testing results from different Test Engines.

Partition Service: It partitions test workloads and assigns them to different Test Engines, according to the computation capacity of each Test Engine.

Adaptive Reliability Calculation of Configurations and Processors Service: It calculates reliability of all returned test results. Similarly, those processors that always return correct test results are treated as reliable processors. The test results from reliable processors have higher reliability that others.

Hamming Distance Service: It gets those NU configurations from N configurations by calculating Hamming distance based on F configurations. Usually NU configurations have one or two Hamming distance from F configurations.

8.3.4 Runtime Composition, Execution and Scalability

Composition: Assuming the GUI layer has five components, each has three options, as $GUI\ template_1, GUI\ template_2, GUI\ template_3$. The workflow layer has three components, individual request, group request, and select candidate configuration for

Fig. 8.3 Database
integration

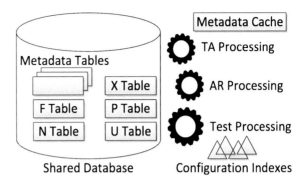

retesting. The service layer has six components: $\otimes$, $\odot$, $\oplus$, partition service, adaptive
reliability calculation, and Hamming distance. The data layer has five types of data,
X, F, P, N, and U.

Two tenants, $Tenant_1$ and $Tenant_2$, use these components to compose their own
applications. $Tenant_1$ chooses $GUI\ template_1$, $text\ font_2$, $text\ size_2$, individual
request, $\otimes$, $\odot$, $\oplus$, F, P, and U. $Tenant_2$ chooses $GUI\ template_3$, $text\ color_2$,
$background\ color_1$, group request, select candidate configuration for retesting, $\otimes$,
$\odot$, $\oplus$, partition service, adaptive reliability calculation, all data types.

Tenant Application Execution: When a tenant request comes in, the TaaS will see
if the tenant application is in the memory. If it is, the tenant application will be called.
If the tenant application is not in the memory, the tenant application metadata will be
retrieved so that tenant application components can be retrieved from the database,
the tenant application will be composed, and then compiled, the executable code will
be deployed to a processor.

Assuming, three processors are available, $Tenant_1$'s TaaS processes can be executed in one machine. $Tenant_2$'s TaaS processes group requests. More test workloads
and five test result statuses are involved in group requests. Partition service splits the
workloads into three parts. Each part is executed on different machines.

As same configurations may be tested by multiple processors, all returned test
results need to be checked by adaptive reliability calculation.

Scalability: The load balancer will assign different workloads to balance the processors. Each processor has stateless servers. Workloads at processors can also be
migrated to another processor to resume computation. Furthermore, the shared database allow each processor to access the data.

8.4 Experimental Results

A group of simulations have been performed, and this section provides one SaaS example for testing. The SaaS has four layers, and each layer has five components, and each component has two options as the initial settings. When the current workloads are finished reaching to 20%, one new component is added to each layer until each layer has ten components. The experiments are done for t-way configurations for $2 \leq t \leq 6$.

The initial settings of infeasible, faulty, and irrelevant configurations are shown in Table 8.2. The number of candidate configurations from five components to ten components each layer are also shown in Table 8.2. When new components are added, the infeasible, faulty, and irrelevant rate are 2%, 0.0003%, and 3% respectively. There are total eight VMs with same computation capacity in this simulation. It supposes that the maximum computation capacity of each VM is 50,000,000 configurations. There two thresholds, $threshold_{min}$ is 20,000,000 configurations (20% of the maximum), and $threshold_{max}$ is 35,000,000 configurations (75% of the maximum). When the workloads of each VM is greater than $threshold_{max}$, new VM will be assigned. When the workloads of each VM is less than $threshold_{min}$, workloads of this VM will be assigned to others, and this VM will stop working. It assumes that when 20% of current workloads are finished, new component will be added to each layer until each layer has ten components.

There are six attempts in total from five components to ten components of each layer. Figure 8.4 shows the number of VMs used in each attempt. When the number of components in each layer increases, the trend is that more VMs are required to process the workloads. From five components to seven components, only one VM is used. The number of components in each layer increases to eight, nine, and ten, the corresponding numbers of VMs are two, four, and eight respectively. Figure 8.5 shows the average computation time of each VM in each attempt. The computation time is counted in seconds. Similarly, when the workloads increase, more execution time of each VM spends. From six to seven components, there is one big gap between the execution times of two VMs. Since only one VM is used to process six or seven components, more workloads are added when six component increases to seven components, more execution times are spent. When nine components increase to ten, the average computation time slightly decreases. Since four more VMs are used when it has ten components in each layer, the average workloads of each VM decreases and its corresponding execution time also decreases.

Based on the proposed TaaS design, when workloads increase, the current working mechanism can be extended. More VMs are added, including test engines, TA Analyzers, AR Analyzers. TaaS scalability issues involving redundancy and recovery, and data migration can be solved in the proposed design. The returned test results from each VM can be shared to other VMs through the current test results sharing mechanism.

Table 8.2 The initial settings of configurations

w.	Size			5 Com	6 Com	7 Com	8 Com	9 Com	10 Com
	X	F	N						
2	5	15	20	760	1,104	1,512	1,984	2,520	3,120
3	50	5	200	9,120	16,192	26,208	39,680	57,120	79,040
4	500	0	2,000	77,520	1.70×10^5	3.28×10^5	5.75×10^5	9.42×10^5	1.46×10^6
5	5,000	0	2×10^4	4.96×10^5	1.36×10^6	3.14×10^6	6.44×10^6	1.21×10^7	2.11×10^7
6	5×10^4	1	2×10^5	2.48×10^6	8.61×10^6	2.41×10^7	5.80×10^7	1.25×10^8	2.46×10^8

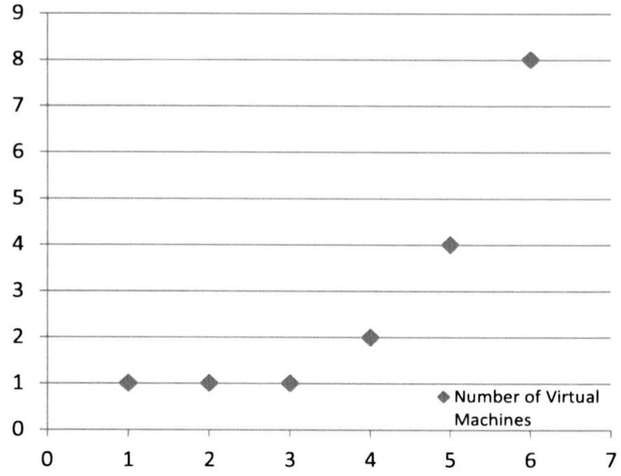

Fig. 8.4 The number of virtual machines of each attempt

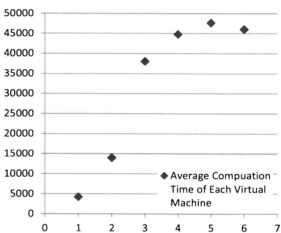

Fig. 8.5 Average computation time of each virtual machine of each attempt

8.5   Conclusion

This chapter talks about TaaS architecture and design. New issues introduced by cloud are discussed and three generations of TaaS are proposed. A TaaS framework has been proposed. TaaS as one type of SaaS can be used to test SaaS. This chapter illustrates the process of using TaaS to test SaaS.

References

1. J. Gao, X. Bai, W.T. Tsai, Cloud testing-issues, challenges, needs and practice. Softw. Eng.: Int. J. (SEIJ), IGI Global **1**, 9–23 (2011)
2. L.M. Riungu, O. Taipale, K. Smolander, Software testing as an online service: observations from practice, in *Proceedings of ICST Workshops*, pp. 418–423, 2010

3. W.-T. Tsai, Y. Huang, X. Bai, J. Gao, Scalable architecture for SaaS, in *Proceedings of 15th IEEE International Symposium on Object Component Service-Oriented Real-time Distributed Computing*, ISORC '12, 2012
4. W.T. Tsai, G. Qi, L. Yu, J. Gao, TaaS (Testing-as-a-Service) design for combinatorial testing, in *Proceedings of IEEE Eighth International Conference on Software Security and Reliability (SERE2014)* (IEEE, 2014), pp. 127–136
5. W. Wu, W.-T. Tsai, C. Jin, G. Qi, J. Luo, Test-algebra execution in a cloud environment, in *Proceedings of 8th IEEE International Symposium on Service-Oriented System Engineering (SOSE2014)*, 2014

Chapter 9
Integrated Taas with Fault Detection and Test Algebra

Abstract Testing-as-a-Service (TaaS) is a software testing service in a cloud that can leverage the computation power provided by the cloud. Specifically, a TaaS can be scaled to large and dynamic workloads, executed in a distributed environment with hundreds of thousands of processors, and these processors may support concurrent and distributed test execution and analysis. This chapter proposes a TaaS system based on AR and TA for combinatorial testing (CT). AR performs testing and identifies faulty interactions, and TA eliminates related configurations from testing and there can be carried out concurrently. By combining these two, it is possible to perform large CT that was not possible before. Specifically, experiments with 2^{50} components with $2.83 * 10^{87}$ 6-way interactions with about $2^{1.1*10^{15}}$ configurations were performed, and this may be the largest CT experimentation as of 2014. 98.6% of configurations have been eliminated out of total number of configurations.

9.1 Framework

9.1.1 Integrated Process

Based on the previous discussion, the incremental and integrated process is proposed as shown in Fig. 9.1 [3, 4, 6]. In the framework, AR runs test configurations to find those F configurations first. AR analysis stops until all F configurations are identified. The identified analyzed F configurations are used by TA to eliminate those X, F, and N configurations from candidate configuration set. TA analysis stops until all X, F, and N configurations are eliminated. After candidate configuration set is analyzed by AR and TA, new components are added. Then TA analyzes the candidate configuration set with new components to eliminate those X, F, and N configurations according to existing test results. After that, AR analyzes the candidate configuration set using existing test results. The same analysis process is repeated until all 6-way interactions

---

Parts of this chapter is reprinted from [4], with permission from Elsevier.

© The Author(s) 2017
W. Tsai and G. Qi, *Combinatorial Testing in Cloud Computing*,
SpringerBriefs in Computer Science, https://doi.org/10.1007/978-981-10-4481-6_9

are analyzed. The process stops when the number of N configurations equals to zero, and all X and F configurations are identified.

Algorithm 10 AR & TA Integrated Processing Algorithm

Require:
    X, F, N, P, U configurations
Ensure:
    deduced F configurations, updated U configurations
1: **while** N == 0 && all X, F configurations are identified && no new components **do**
2:   **if** F configuration exist **then**
3:     Run AR
4:     Return identified F interaction
5:   **end if**
6:   **while** all related X, F, and N configurations are eliminated based on existing test results **do**
7:     **if** F interaction ‖ X configuration ‖ N configuration exists && U configuration exists **then**
8:       Run TA
9:       Return identified F configurations & updated U configurations
10:     **end if**
11:     Add new components
12:   **end while**
13: **end while**

Different number of U configurations are sent to each processor to do **TA** analysis according to its computation capacity. When one processor finishes analyzing the assigned U configurations, new U configurations will be assigned. New U configurations are randomly picked from candidate configuration set. The finalized configurations will be updated in test database. Those configurations that cannot be finalized through testing analysis will be tested. The process stops until all U configurations are finalized.

The incremental process is proposed to emulate the SaaS tenant application development process. After a SaaS system is deployed, new tenants can be added, while other tenant applications are being executed at the same time. Each time a new tenant is added, zero or more components will be added with at least one new configuration.

It is possible to add components in a batch mode rather than on a continuous mode to save the incremental computation. It is also possible to run a non-incremental manner where all the components and all required configurations are known.

9.1.2   Framework Illustration

One example is used to illustrate the overall framework. There are six components (a, b, c, d, e, f) and each component has two options. There are total 2^6 configurations. Suppose 2-way combination (c, e) and 6-way combination (a, b, c, d, e, d) are faulty. The initial settings are shown in Table 9.1, involving X, N, and P configurations.

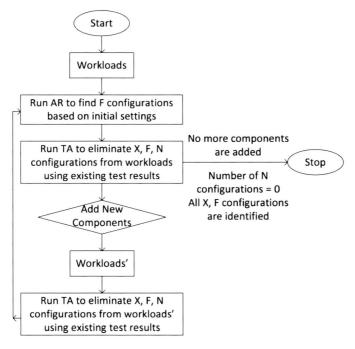

Fig. 9.1 The flowchart of AR and TA analysis

Table 9.1 6-Component example initial settings

	Configurations #	F #	X #	N #	P #
2-way	15	1	0	3	2
3-way	20	0	0	5	3
4-way	15	0	0	0	2
5-way	6	0	1	0	1
6-way	1	1	0	0	0

Step 1: AR analyzes the workloads, based on the initial settings. One test hits 6-way failure and four tests hit 2-way failures. AR stops until all F configurations are identified.

Step 2: Based on the initial settings and the identified F configurations, TA analyzes the candidate set. Four F 3-way configurations, six F 4-way configurations, and four F 5-way configurations are eliminated by TA as shown in Table 9.2. TA stops until all related X, F, and N configurations are eliminated.

Step 3: One new component g is added and workloads increase. Suppose one F 5-way configuration, one F 6-way configuration, and two N 4-way configurations are also

Table 9.2 Related configurations eliminated by TA

	F #	X #	N #	Configurations need to be tested
2-way	1	0	3	9
3-way	4	0	5	8
4-way	6	0	0	7
5-way	4	1	0	0
6-way	1	0	0	0

Table 9.3 Increased configurations by adding new component

	Increased configuration #
2-way	6
3-way	15
4-way	20
5-way	15
6-way	6

Table 9.4 Related configurations eliminated by TA

	F #	N #	Configurations need to be tested
2-way	0	0	6
3-way	1	0	14
4-way	4	2	14
5-way	6	0	9
6-way	0	0	6

added in the increased configurations. The increased number of configurations are shown in Table 9.3.

Step 4: Based on the existing test results, TA analyzes the candidate configuration set. One F 3-way configuration, four F 4-way configurations, and six F 5-way configurations are eliminated as shown in Table 9.4. TA stops until all related X, F, and N configurations are eliminated.

Step 5: Based on existing test results, AR analyzes those configurations in candidate configuration set. Four test cases hit 5-way failure and three test cases hit 6-way failure. AR stops until all F configurations are identified.

Step 6: Based on the existing test results and the new identified F configurations, TA analyzes the candidate configuration set. One F 5-way configuration and three F 6-way configurations are eliminated by TA as shown in Table 9.5. TA stops until all related X, F, and N configurations are eliminated.

Table 9.5 Related configurations eliminated by TA

	F #	Configurations need to be tested
2-way	0	6
3-way	0	14
4-way	0	14
5-way	1	8
6-way	3	3

Step 7: No more components are added. All X and F configurations are eliminated from candidate configuration set. And no N configuration is in the candidate set. The integrated process stops.

9.2 Experiments and Results

9.2.1 Experiment Setup

To evaluate the integrated process including its scalability, we performed extensive simulations, this section provides five large experiments with 2^{10}, 2^{20}, 2^{30}, 2^{40}, and 2^{50} components, and each component has two options. The corresponding number of configurations are $2^{2^{10}} = 2^{1024} = 1.79*10^{308}$, $2^{2^{20}}$, $2^{2^{30}}$, $2^{2^{40}}$, and $2^{2^{50}}$, furthermore $2^{2^{10}} \ll 2^{2^{20}} \ll 2^{2^{30}} \ll 2^{2^{40}} \ll 2^{2^{50}}$.

Tables 9.6, 9.7, 9.8, 9.9, 9.10 show the number of components and configurations. For example, 2^{50} components will have $2.83*10^{87}$ 6-way configurations. Compare to previously reported experiments [1, 2, 7], this may be the largest experimentation size in CT known to the authors as of 2014.

To visualize the growth of configurations, Fig. 9.2 shows the increased workloads when the number of components increases, each time the total number of configurations increases exponentially. Based on the initial seeded faults, each configuration from 2-way to 6-way (up to $2.83*10^{87}$) is analyzed.

Tables 9.6, 9.7, 9.8, 9.9, 9.10 show the number of all involved configurations from 2-way to 6-way, initial setting of X, N, and P configurations, respectively, for 2^{10}, 2^{20}, 2^{30}, 2^{40}, and 2^{50} components.

Note that F configurations have been set up for a challenging situation where few faults are seeded for 3-way to 6-way interactions, and in some cases no-fault is seeded, especially in the light of the enormous size of t-way configurations in these systems. For example, out of $2.45*10^{59}$, only one fault is seeded as a 6-way fault in 2^{40} system. In this case, AR will need to test many configurations to encounter a failure, and as few F configurations are available, TA will not be efficient in eliminating configurations.

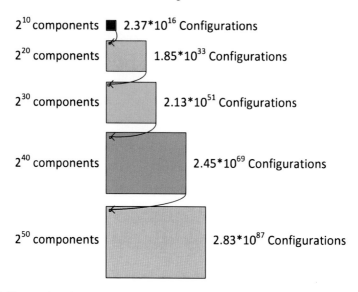

2^{10} components ■ $2.37*10^{16}$ Configurations

2^{20} components $1.85*10^{33}$ Configurations

2^{30} components $2.13*10^{51}$ Configurations

2^{40} components $2.45*10^{69}$ Configurations

2^{50} components $2.83*10^{87}$ Configurations

Fig. 9.2 The number of components in TaaS simulation

Table 9.6 Initial 2^{10} components experiment setups

	Configs #	F Configs by AR	X Configs	N Configs	P Configs
2-way	523,776	10	524	348,311	149,276
3-way	$5.35*10^8$	2	$5.35*10^5$	$3.51*10^8$	$1.49*10^8$
4-way	$2.73*10^{11}$	0	$2.73*10^8$	$1.78*10^{11}$	$7.70*10^{10}$
5-way	$9.29*10^{13}$	0	$9.29*10^{10}$	$6.07*10^{13}$	$2.61*10^{13}$
6-way	$2.37*10^{16}$	1	$2.37*10^{13}$	$1.54*10^{16}$	$6.64*10^{15}$

Table 9.7 Initial 2^{20} components experiment setups

	Configs #	F Configs by AR	X Configs	N Configs	P Configs
2-way	$5.50*10^{11}$	10,486	$5.50*10^8$	$3.59*10^{11}$	$1.55*10^{11}$
3-way	$1.92*10^{17}$	4	$1.92*10^{14}$	$1.25*10^{17}$	$5.51*10^{16}$
4-way	$5.03*10^{22}$	1	$5.03*10^{19}$	$3.29*10^{22}$	$1.41*10^{22}$
5-way	$1.06*10^{28}$	1	$1.06*10^{25}$	$6.93*10^{27}$	$2.97*10^{27}$
6-way	$1.85*10^{33}$	1	$1.85*10^{30}$	$1.20*10^{33}$	$5.20*10^{32}$

Table 9.8 Initial 2^{30} components experiment setups

	Configs #	F Configs by AR	X Configs	N Configs	P Configs
2-way	$5.76*10^{17}$	$1.07*10^{7}$	$5.76*10^{15}$	$3.76*10^{17}$	$1.62*10^{17}$
3-way	$2.06*10^{26}$	10	$2.06*10^{24}$	$1.34*10^{26}$	$5.81*10^{25}$
4-way	$5.54*10^{34}$	2	$5.54*10^{32}$	$3.61*10^{34}$	$1.56*10^{34}$
5-way	$1.19*10^{43}$	2	$1.19*10^{41}$	$7.71*10^{42}$	$3.34*10^{42}$
6-way	$2.13*10^{51}$	1	$2.13*10^{49}$	$1.39*10^{51}$	$6.02*10^{50}$

Table 9.9 Initial 2^{40} components experiment setups

	Configs #	F Configs by AR	X Configs	N Configs	P Configs
2-way	$6.04*10^{23}$	$1.10*10^{10}$	$6.04*10^{21}$	$3.94*10^{23}$	$1.70*10^{23}$
3-way	$2.22*10^{35}$	23	$2.22*10^{33}$	$1.44*10^{35}$	$6.32*10^{34}$
4-way	$6.09*10^{46}$	4	$6.09*10^{44}$	$3.98*10^{46}$	$1.71*10^{46}$
5-way	$1.34*10^{58}$	2	$1.34*10^{56}$	$8.75*10^{57}$	$3.75*10^{57}$
6-way	$2.45*10^{69}$	1	$2.45*10^{67}$	$1.60*10^{69}$	$6.93*10^{68}$

Table 9.10 Initial 2^{50} components experiment setups

	Configs #	F Configs by AR	X Configs	N Configs	P Configs
2-way	$6.34*10^{29}$	$1.13*10^{13}$	$6.34*10^{27}$	$4.14*10^{29}$	$1.78*10^{29}$
3-way	$2.38*10^{44}$	35	$2.38*10^{42}$	$1.55*10^{44}$	$6.67*10^{43}$
4-way	$6.70*10^{58}$	5	$6.70*10^{56}$	$4.38*10^{58}$	$1.88*10^{58}$
5-way	$1.51*10^{73}$	3	$1.51*10^{71}$	$9.87*10^{72}$	$4.23*10^{72}$
6-way	$2.83*10^{87}$	1	$2.83*10^{85}$	$1.84*10^{87}$	$8.04*10^{86}$

In the simulation, 500 candidate configurations are sent to each processor one time. When 450 configurations are processed, another 500 candidate configurations are added to each processor. Figure 9.3 shows the nature of concurrent AR and TA tasks in the integrated process. At the beginning, only AR can execute as it needs to identify F or X first. When AR identifies a failure, the faulty interactions

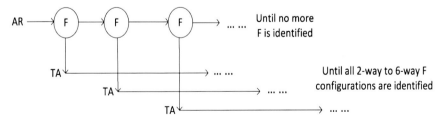

Fig. 9.3 The integrated process

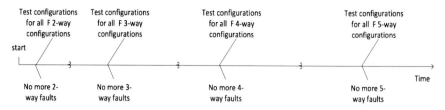

Fig. 9.4 AR test configurations to identify all T-way faults ($2 \leq T \leq 5$)

can be quickly identified by reasoning, and once the faulty interaction is identified, TA will initiate a new concurrent process to eliminate related faulty interactions automatically. When AR detects the second failure and second fault interactions, TA may not have completed its execution, and thus another TA process is initiated based on the newly identified faulty interactions. In this way, numerous TA processes can be executed at the same time with the AR process. Multiple AR processes can be executed too, but each takes different configuration for testing. Each TA process will stop when all related F configurations from 2-way to 6-way are identified. As all these processes share the same database, any update done by any concurrent TA processes will be available to the AR process immediately, TA rules ensures that any results obtained by TA will be eventually consistent regardless if the same configuration may be identified multiple times. For example, combination (a, b) is faulty, so is (c, d), then configuration (a, b, c, d) will be identified by two TA processes, one from (a, b), the other (c, d), but both processes will produce consistent results.

Furthermore, as the number of components increases, the number of F, X, N, and P configurations also increases, and for the same number of components, the number of X, N, and P configurations increases from 2-way to 6-way.

Another important consideration is that each initial F and X seeded are unique. For example, if combination (a, b) is a seeded 2-way fault, then (a, b, c) cannot be an initial 3-way fault for any component c, nor it can be a 3-way X combination. By arranging the initial F and X seeded in this manner, these can be detected by AR only, not by TA. Otherwise, if (a, b, c) is also seeded, TA will pick it up when it detects that (a, b) is a F, and eliminated it automatically. Thus, the initial X and F seeded have been carefully designed so that they can be detected by AR only to evaluate the integrated process under a challenging situation.

All simulations are run on four Intel Xeon processor E7-4870 v2 (30M Cache, 2.30 GHz, 15 cores) machines. Then machines run for about a month on a dedicated mode for the experiments.

9.2.2 Experiment Results

The following results are obtained:

- Each experiment has been run 3 times, and all the results are presented with the average of three runs;
- All 2-way to 6-way faults seeded have been identified by AR in all these experiments;
- All the identified 2-way to 6-way faults have been used by TA to eliminate as many corresponding configurations;
- All the experiments have been conducted using incremental process as stated in Sect. 9.1 until there is no more N configurations, i.e., the system runs out of new configuration for testing.
- Hundreds of thousand TA analysis run concurrently.
- $N_c = N_{xta} + N_{far} + N_{fta} + N_{nta} + N_p + N_u$. N_c is the total number of t-way configurations ($2 \leq t \leq 6$). N_{xta} is the number of X t-way configurations eliminated by TA. N_{far} and N_{fta} are the number of F t-way configurations identified by AR and eliminated by TA respectively. N_{nta} is the number of N t-way configurations eliminated by TA. N_p is the number of P t-way configurations. N_u is the number of U t-way configurations.

Figure 9.4 shows the number of test configurations need to identify all t-way faults ($2 \leq t \leq 5$) by AR. Note that these are different from those configurations eliminated by TA. These initial seeded faults can be identified by AR only due to the unique design described in the previous subsection. As few faults are seeded in 3-way to 6-way interactions, the numbers of test configurations needed for AR are large.

9.2.3 Measurements

N_{tc}: **the number of t-way configurations needed to identify a t-way fault, and versus the total number of t-way configurations**. Tables 9.11 and 9.12 show the number of configurations from 2-way to 6-way in identifying faults and the related percentage over corresponding configurations from 2-way to 6-way. For example, in the case 2^{10} 2-way interaction faults, AR needs to perform 2,340 tests on average to hit ten failures, and this is only 0.45% of all 2-way possible configurations. While the number of configurations needed increases with increasing components, but the percentage becomes smaller rapidly. In fact, only $2.54*10^{-67}$% of 3-way configurations will be needed. If one compares the ratio but using the total number of configurations (rather than 3-way configurations), the ratio will be even smaller. In general, AR needs to perform a tiny fraction of the total number of t-way configurations of $2 \leq t \leq 6$.

Number of t-way interaction eliminated: TA eliminated any 2-way to 6-way F configurations caused by seeded 2-way to 6-way faults, and this is shown in Table 9.13.

Fig. 9.5 Total workloads and testing workloads saved

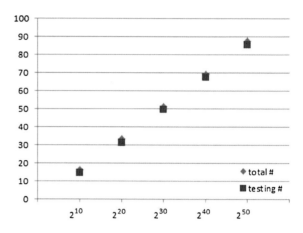

Similarly, the X configurations eliminated by TA and their ratio to the total number t-way configurations are shown in Table 9.14. For each fault identified, a huge number of configurations are eliminated on average. For example, while only 2 faults are seeded in 3-way interactions in 2^{30} system, $6.19*10^{24}$ configurations are eliminated by TA. This shows that while AR needs to perform many tests to identify an interaction fault, but each interaction fault identified can lead to significant reduction in overall test workloads. As the number of components increases, the reduction is even more significant. The total number of configurations eliminated by the integrated process are shown in Table 9.15.

Table 9.16 shows the number of configurations that need to be tested and the corresponding percentage of the total number of configurations, and the results showed that consistently only about 1.6% of configuration need to be tested, or about 98.4% of configurations do not needed to be tested.

An interesting question is about the consistency of 1.6% as similar results were obtained using different parameters on smaller scale systems [5, 7]. This percentage does not go down or up significantly regardless of the experiment size.

Figure 9.5 shows the total workloads and testing workloads saved plotted using a logarithmic graph. Based on the initial settings, the number of components from 2^{10} to 2^{50} have more 98.3% deduction rate that is shown in Fig. 9.6.

R_{ec}:**the ratio of the eliminated configurations over total number of configurations**. Table 9.17 shows TA deduction efficiency. When the number of components increases, the efficiency always keeps at the same level. The deduction rate increases from 2-way configurations to 6-way configurations.

The deduction rate with N configurations is higher than the deduction rate without N configurations. N configuration is one key factor to affect the TA efficiency. When the number of N configurations increases, TA analysis is more efficient.

Computational complexity needed to eliminate those faulty t-way configurations for $2 \leq t \leq 6$: All related F or X configurations up to 6-way are eliminated from testing considerations by TA analysis, according to the initial F or X seeded interactions.

Table 9.11 Test configurations # of identifying faults in 2-way to 6-way configurations

Components	2^{10}	2^{20}	2^{30}	2^{40}	2^{50}
	Test configurations				
2-way	2,340	$4.39*10^6$	$6.67*10^9$	$9.10*10^{12}$	$1.17*10^{16}$
3-way	1,334	5,816	24,370	82,156	$1.66*10^5$
4-way	na	4,285	6,941	78,896	40,755
5-way	na	12,138	19,871	57,666	38,376

Table 9.12 Percentage of test configurations over 2-way to 6-way configurations

Components	2^{10}	2^{20}	2^{30}	2^{40}	2^{50}
	Percentage (%)				
2-way	0.45	0.000798	$1.16*10^{-6}$	$1.51*10^{-9}$	$1.85*10^{-12}$
3-way	0.000249	$3.03*10^{-12}$	$1.18*10^{-20}$	$3.70*10^{-29}$	$6.97*10^{-38}$
4-way	na	$8.52*10^{-18}$	$1.25*10^{-29}$	$1.30*10^{-40}$	$6.08*10^{-53}$
5-way	na	$1.15*10^{-22}$	$1.67*10^{-37}$	$4.30*10^{-52}$	$2.54*10^{-67}$

Table 9.13 F configurations deduction by TA

Components	2^{10}	2^{20}	2^{30}	2^{40}	2^{50}
	Deducted F				
2-way	10	10,486	$1.07*10^7$	$1.10*10^{10}$	$1.13*10^{13}$
3-way	10,222	$1.10*10^{10}$	$1.15*10^{16}$	$1.21*10^{22}$	$1.27*10^{28}$
4-way	$5.22*10^6$	$5.76*10^{15}$	$6.19*10^{24}$	$6.65*10^{33}$	$7.14*10^{42}$
5-way	$1.77*10^9$	$2.01*10^{21}$	$2.22*10^{33}$	$2.44*10^{45}$	$2.68*10^{57}$
6-way	$4.52*10^{11}$	$5.27*10^{26}$	$5.95*10^{41}$	$6.70*10^{56}$	$7.54*10^{71}$

Table 9.14 X configurations deduction by TA

Components	2^{10}	2^{20}	2^{30}	2^{40}	2^{50}
	Deducted X				
2-way	524	$5.50*10^8$	$5.76*10^{15}$	$6.04*10^{21}$	$6.34*10^{27}$
3-way	$2.08*10^7$	$6.79*10^{15}$	$6.59*10^{24}$	$6.92*10^{33}$	$7.85*10^{42}$
4-way	$1.27*10^{10}$	$2.32*10^{21}$	$2.12*10^{33}$	$2.27*10^{45}$	$2.49*10^{57}$
5-way	$4.44*10^{12}$	$5.10*10^{26}$	$5.31*10^{41}$	$5.41*10^{56}$	$5.97*10^{71}$
6-way	$1.25*10^{15}$	$9.79*10^{31}$	$8.19*10^{49}$	$9.26*10^{67}$	$1.12*10^{86}$

Table 9.15 Configurations eliminated by AR & TA

Number of components	Configurations eliminated	Percentage (%)
2^{10}	$2.33*10^{16}$	98.34
2^{20}	$1.82*10^{33}$	98.34
2^{30}	$2.10*10^{51}$	98.38
2^{40}	$2.41*10^{69}$	98.39
2^{50}	$2.78*10^{87}$	98.39

Table 9.16 Configurations need to be tested

Number of components	Configurations need to be tested	Percentage
2^{10}	$3.93*10^{14}$	1.66
2^{20}	$3.14*10^{31}$	1.66
2^{30}	$3.45*10^{49}$	1.62
2^{40}	$3.94*10^{67}$	1.61
2^{50}	$4.56*10^{85}$	1.61

Table 9.17 TA deduction rate

Components	2^{10} (%)	2^{20} (%)	2^{30} (%)	2^{40} (%)	2^{50} (%)
2-way	96.32	96.32	96.33	96.33	96.33
3-way	97.44	97.44	97.45	97.45	97.45
4-way	98.15	98.15	98.15	98.16	98.16
5-way	98.31	98.31	98.32	98.32	98.33
6-way	98.36	98.37	98.37	98.37	98.37

Table 9.18 Computation steps of TA analysis

Compos	2^{10}	2^{20}	2^{30}	2^{40}	2^{50}
Configs	$2^{2^{10}}$	$2^{2^{20}}$	$2^{2^{30}}$	$2^{2^{40}}$	$2^{2^{50}}$
Steps	$7.79*10^{30}$	$5.54*10^{64}$	$7.68*10^{100}$	$8.68*10^{136}$	$1.28*10^{173}$
Ratio	$4.35*10^{-278}$	approx 0	approx 0	approx 0	approx 0

Regardless of the initial F or X seeded interactions, the worst case is that all the 2-way to 6-way configurations must be visited. For n components, the number of all configurations from 2-way to 6-way is $C_2^n + C_3^n + C_4^n + C_5^n + C_6^n$ with time complexity $O(n^6)$. All F and X configurations from 2-way to 6-way are identified by TA within time complexity $O(n^6)$. While these numbers look large, but when one compares them to the total number of possible configuration, these numbers are actually small as $O(n^6) \ll O(2^n)$. When n increases, the percentage of n^6 over 2^n decreases. $\lim_{n \to infty} \frac{n^6}{2^n} = 0$.

Fig. 9.6 Configuration deduction rate

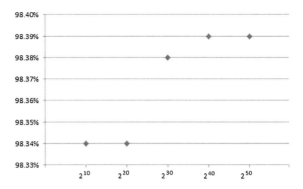

Table 9.18 shows all the computation steps that of TA performed in the simulation to eliminate 2-way to 6-way configurations for 2^{10} to 2^{50} systems, as well as the ratio of the computation steps over the total configuration. One can see that the ratio is almost zero for all these systems, with the largest number being $4.35*10^{-275}$ and it is close to zero already. As TA deals with configuration elimination, not components, thus TA needs to traverse a tiny fraction of the total number of configuration to cover most 2-way to 6-way configurations.

9.3 Conclusion

With the arrival of cloud computing, the need to perform large CT to identify faulty interactions and configurations, instead of just coverage, has also arrived. At the same time, the cloud also provided significant computing resources including CPUs and storage that allow people to perform CT exercises that were not possible before. This chapter has proposed a TaaS framework that allows large CT exercises to detect faulty interactions and configuration in SaaS. The proposed framework combines faulty detection with asynchronous TA to eliminate related configurations concurrently. The goal of this project is to demonstrate that it is possible to run large CT with a huge number (2^{50}) of components with $2^{2^{50}}$ of configurations. This may be the largest CT experiments known to the authors as of 2014 with $2.45*10^{69}$ 6-way configurations alone. The combined process has been simulated using 60 CPUs that run for almost a month on a dedicated mode with a large number of concurrent processes. The process successfully eliminated about 98.4% of test configurations from testing consideration consistent across these experiments. These exercises demonstrated that the proposed TaaS framework can work on large project with large number of components and configurations.

References

1. R. Kuhn, Combinatorial testing (2010), http://csrc.nist.gov/groups/SNS/acts/documents/SP800-142-101006.pdf/
2. R. Kuhn, Y. Lei, R. Kacker, Practical combinatorial testing: beyond pairwise. IT Prof. **10**(3), 19–23 (2008)
3. W.-T. Tsai, G. Qi, Integrated adaptive reasoning testing framework with automated fault detection, in *Proceedings of IEEE Symposium on Service-Oriented System Engineering (SOSE2015)* (IEEE, 2015), pp. 169–178
4. W.-T. Tsai, G. Qi, Integrated fault detection and test algebra for combinatorial testing in taas (testing-as-a-service). Simul. Model. Prac. Theory **68**, 108–124 (2016)
5. W.-T. Tsai, J. Luo, G. Qi, W. Wu, Concurrent test algebra execution with combinatorial testing, in *Proceedings of 8th IEEE International Symposium on Service-Oriented System Engineering (SOSE2014)* (2014)
6. W.-T. Tsai, G. Qi, K. Hu, Autonomous decentralized combinatorial testing, in *Proceedings of IEEE Twelfth International Symposium on Autonomous Decentralized Systems (ISADS2015)* (IEEE, 2015), pp. 40–47
7. W. Wu, W.-T. Tsai, C. Jin, G. Qi, J. Luo, Test-algebra execution in a cloud environment, in *Proceedings of 8th IEEE International Symposium on Service-Oriented System Engineering (SOSE2014)* (2014)